JAMAAL WILKES

MEMOIRS OF *THE ORIGINAL*
SMOOTH AS SILK

with Edward Reynolds Davis JR

Certificate of Registration

This Certificate issued under the seal of the Copyright Office in accordance with title 17, *United States Code*, attests that registration has been made for the work identified below. The information on this certificate has been made a part of the Copyright Office records.

Maria A. Pallante

Register of Copyrights, United States of America

This book is dedicated to
the loving memory of my sister.

L. Naomi Wilkes, Esq.

April 4, 1950–March 12, 1993
An Inspiration
and
My Guardian Angel

TABLE OF CONTENTS

UCLA All-Americans Bill Walton and Jamaal Keith Wilkes

A SPECIAL MESSAGE
By Bill Walton

HALL OF FAME, 1993

This is the proudest moment in my entire life, as today I have the unique honor, privilege, and distinction of writing a special message for the autobiography of "Jamaal Wilkes, Memoirs of the Original Smooth As Silk."

I have known Jamaal for nearly forty years. The forces that shaped the greatest dynasty in the history of intercollegiate athletics, the UCLA Bruins, brought us together. The coaching staff at UCLA, John Wooden (Hall of Fame '60 and '73) and Denny Crum (Hall of Fame '94) had identified a fifteen-year-old, reed-thin son of a Baptist minister and social worker from Santa Barbara, California, one Jamaal Wilkes, as a core member of their next great team.

I had the opportunity and pleasure to play alongside Jamaal for four years in Westwood, in addition to sitting right next to him, not only in the classroom, library, and church but also in that greatest of sanctuaries, the UCLA locker room. Over the decades, we have become and remained the best of friends.

In support of Jamaal's body of work on and off the basketball court, it is important to realize that the two nicest and most important things that anyone could ever say about a real ballplayer describe Jamaal and his game perfectly. At the very top of Coach Wooden's Pyramid of Success, the capstone block is Competitive Greatness, which is defined as doing your best when your best is needed. Additionally, Jamaal made everyone he ever played with a vastly superior player.

Jamaal Wilkes was a perfect player, and he is an even finer person. He could do anything and everything. He game was complete and flawless. He could play offense and defense. He could run, pass, shoot, catch, dribble, defend, and rebound, and his footwork was impeccable. He was an essential component on teams that are generally considered and acknowledged as the best ever.

On offense, Jamaal was a regular and consistent scorer and the sure place to go whenever you really needed something good to happen.

On defense, Jamaal always guarded the best of the best—with typically phenomenal results.

Jamaal was not a player who relied on athletic prowess, unusual size or strength, or any physical superiority. His game was based on all the human attributes and personal characteristics that are embodied in Wooden's pyramid. Jamaal always found himself matched up against the other team's greatest players. Including David Thompson (Hall of Fame '96), to Julius Erving (Hall of Fame '93), to Larry Bird (Hall of Fame

'98), to Dominique Wilkins (Hall of Fame '06), the list is endless. Yet it was Jamaal's team that almost always came out on top. This was not a coincidence.

Jamaal had an admittedly unorthodox delivery to his pure-as-can-be jump shot. When John Wooden, arguably the greatest teacher that the game of basketball has ever known, was queried about how he, Coach Wooden, could possibly tolerate such a blatant disregard for the textbook execution of the most basic and elementary part of the game, Wooden always was quick to point out, "If Jamaal ever starts missing any of those shots, then I'll have a chat with him about it." That conversation never took place.

Later on as professional, when Jamaal was playing for the Los Angeles Lakers in the NBA, Chick Hearn (Hall of Fame '03), the voice of the Los Angeles Lakers for many years, coined yet another perfectly appropriate phrase that described Jamaal. When Jamaal got the ball for a perimeter jump shot, during the release of the ball, Chick would always say, "Wilkes, for the twenty-foot layup," and that's the way it was. Never forget that Chick Hearn is the only media member to ever be enshrined into the Naismith Memorial Basketball Hall of Fame.

Jamaal Wilkes played on some of the greatest teams, with some of the greatest players, and in most of the biggest games of his era. He was inevitably and invariably on the winning side. It is safe to say that the championships followed Jamaal wherever he went.

At UCLA—where Jamaal was a member of two NCAA title-winning squads, on an undefeated freshman team, and part of the historic eighty-eight-game winning streak, as well as being a key contributor to UCLA's NCAA Tournament—record winning streak of thirty-eight consecutive games—Jamaal played in the first ever Monday night NCAA Championship game—a game where he was the Bruins' second highest scorer, with sixteen points.

While attending UCLA from 1970–1974, Jamaal was also a three-time academic all-American. He is already enshrined in the Academic All-America Hall of Fame (class of '90).

When Jamaal graduated with honors from UCLA, he was the eleventh player chosen in the 1974 NBA draft, picked by the Golden State Warriors, where Al Attles (Hall of Fame of Life) coached him. In 1975, Jamaal went on to win Rookie of the Year honors that initial season of his twelve-year NBA career, and he and teammate Rick Barry (Hall of Fame '87) led the Warriors to their only NBA title. In the finals that year, in typical Jamaal Wilkes style and fashion, he completely outplayed and dominated Elvin Hayes (Hall of Fame '90) as the Warriors, playing without the home-court advantage, swept the heavily favored Washington Bullets. It must be noted that Jamaal remains, to this very day, one of the lowest drafted players to ever win Rookie of the Year honors.

Jamaal then went on to play for the Los Angeles Lakers, where, not surprisingly, he was on three more NBA-title teams. There, under the tutelage of soon-to-be Hall of Fame coach Pat Riley (Hall of Fame '08) and teaming up with Kareem Abdul-Jabbar (Hall of Fame '95) and Magic Johnson (Hall of Fame '02), the Lakers and their Showtime attack captivated fans around the globe and defined what it meant to play great ball.

In game six of the 1980 NBA Finals on the road in Philadelphia, when Kareem could not play because of injury, in a game that many remember for the brilliance of Magic Johnson, never discount the historical fact that Jamaal Wilkes was the second leading scorer for the champion Lakers that night. With thirty-seven points (twenty-five in the second and decisive half) to go along with his ten rebounds, Jamaal took it to, through, and beyond the incomparable Dr. J.

And while Jamaal might be somewhat overlooked by Magic's special performance that night in Philadelphia—much the same way that Walt Frazier's (Hall of Fame '87) magnificent game seven in the 1970 NBA Championship is often overshadowed by the emotional heroics of Willis Reed (Hall of Fame '82)— the records and accomplishments of Jamaal Wilkes stand alone for this former two-time NCAA Champion and all-American, four-time NBA Champion, and three-time NBA All-Star.

Jamaal Wilkes is one of only five players in the history of all basketball to have won multiple NCAA and NBA championships. All five are in the Naismith Memorial Basketball Hall of Fame: Bill Russell ('75), K.C. Jones ('89), Kareem, and me ('93). That, my friends, is pretty good company.

But more importantly than any recitation of the statistics that make Jamaal Wilkes an easy and clear choice as a Hall of Famer, it are his hands, his heart, and his soul that separate him from the crowd.

Jamaal could catch anything. All you had to do was throw it anywhere in his direction, and he would turn maybe the worst pass ever thrown into a masterful thing of beauty. It is not without the receiver that the credit for being a great passer is bestowed. Jamaal Wilkes played alongside those who are generally regarded as history's greatest passers.

Jamaal's sense of humanity already put him in life's Hall of Fame. With his humble, caring, selfless, sharing, quiet demeanor and personality, Jamaal has all the positive personality traits that you could ever want or hope for in any one human being. Unselfishness is a staple of teaching young kids the game of basketball, and no one was better at it than Jamaal.

Jamaal Wilkes is the one player who every coach he ever played for lights up whenever his name is mentioned.

But Jamaal is never one to trumpet his own cause; he is always about the team and what he can possibly do to make the squad better.

Jamaal Wilkes is the person and player that we can all only dream of becoming.

In a world gone mad before our eyes—a world of hype, self-promotion, and out-of-control ego—Jamaal Wilkes is a beacon of hope that, maybe, justice will be served.

And that is why I write this special message.

I

THE UCLA BRUIN LEGACY

As freshmen, we didn't come into much contact with Coach Wooden. Coach Wooden, however, did stop by to watch our practices from time to time. I could see that he was studying my unorthodox jump shot. I could feel he had some thoughts about suggesting a change. But he and the coaching staff came to the conclusion that, as long as I had a good backspin on the ball, they could live with the way I shot the jumper and free throws.

The UCLA Bruins were coming off of their fourth consecutive NCAA championship as my class arrived on campus in Westwood, a ritzy area of Los Angeles nestled between Beverly Hills, Bel Air, West Los Angeles, and Santa Monica and bounded by Sunset Boulevard to the north, Wilshire Boulevard to the south, Beverly Glen Boulevard to the east, and the San Diego Freeway

(405) to the west. I stepped onto campus after the first championship in the post–Kareem Abdul-Jabbar (Lew Alcindor) era.

The championship victory came against Jacksonville State, 80-69. Three Bruins were named to the all-tournament team: Sidney Wicks, Curtis Rowe, and John Vallely. The game was a John Wooden masterpiece in which he assigned Wicks to guard the imposing seven-foot-two-inch Artis "The A Train" Gilmore of Jacksonville. Gilmore, perhaps, was the most dominating player in college basketball and posed a major challenge to the Bruins, but Wicks—at six feet, eight inches—proved to be the better athlete.

It was a classic example of the coaching strategies that made John Wooden a Hall of Fame coach. Typical of Coach Wooden, he knew he held a high trump card with Wicks, who not only was an all-American but a veteran of three NCAA championship games.

Vallely was the only player departing from that team, so the championship streak appeared to be in good hands until my freshman class would ascend to center court.

The UCLA freshman basketball coach was Gary Cunningham, who was also the academic counselor. Coach Cunningham's assistant was Jim Nielsen. Another academic counselor who worked closely with the basketball team was the late Laura Brown, who helped us select classes to keep us on track earn a degree in four years.

Since I was actually new to Los Angeles proper, it helped that I didn't really know or like the city. I just stayed on campus and studied. I found the city too busy and freeways too complicated. I developed a very private lifestyle. Being studious and private, I was able to stay away from the Bruin hoopla for the most part.

My most exciting social outings were going over to the apartment of my sister Naomi, who was in law school at USC, or to Pasadena with my roommate and UCLA teammate Vince Carson.

Vince and I were two of six high-school all-Americans on the freshmen basketball team. Vince had attended Muir High School in Pasadena. Then there were Greg Lee and Gary Franklin from Reseda High School, a Los Angeles city school in the San Fernando Valley; Hank Babcock of Notre Dame High School, a private school in the San Fernando Valley; and Bill Walton from San Diego.

Tommy Curtis from Tallahassee, Florida, a redshirt the previous year, practiced with both the freshmen and the varsity teams.

New to the varsity that year was Larry Hollyfield, the CIF Southern Section Player of the Year the year before me and a tremendously gifted athlete at Compton High School, where he was 62–0 as a starter. He was transferring from a Compton Community College team that went 33–0 the year before. This meant that Larry was 95–0 as a starter when he arrived at UCLA. When he left, he still was undefeated as a starter.

There were other two redshirt players joining the varsity, Martin Vitatoe and Bob Webb.

John Vallely was one of the premiere point guards in college basketball, but fortunately it was just the one personnel loss.

As a unit, we didn't really interact a great deal with the varsity. Bill, however, practiced with them a lot. I did develop a good personal relationship with Sidney Wicks and Curtis Rowe, the two big stars of the varsity team. I had gotten to know them during the recruitment visit.

They took me under their wings and looked out for me the first year. I got to meet and know the Wicks family pretty well. Both Sidney and Curtis were from South-Central Los Angeles.

I was really impressed with the extremely close relationship Sidney and Curtis had. Both were fierce competitors at rival Los Angeles City high schools. Now they were closer than brothers.

As freshmen and non-varsity players, we were removed, somewhat, from all the UCLA college basketball-dynasty hoopla. We were, however, aware that we were the ones who would be stepping into the shoes of the varsity players and that it was just a matter of exactly who the key players would be.

It was clear right off the bat that Bill would be the kingpin. He practiced with the varsity to get accustomed to the championship caliber of play, the more physical level of the game, and the increased intensity that did not exist among the competition we faced with our freshman schedule of mostly junior college teams.

Our practices were very well scheduled, to which we tightly adhered. We could see that UCLA basketball, behind the scenes, was a class act.

At UCLA, under Coach Wooden, little things were big things. In actuality, they were the things that *seemed little*, but the more you learned, understood, and practiced, they became big things.

One of those was the utilization of the bank shot.

I learned to appreciate the use of the angles on the square of the backboard above the hoop. In many ways, basketball is like geometry. Whether it's the angle you're shooting from for a bank shot or the angle at which you are making a leading bounce pass down court, geometry definitely comes into play.

Bob Swanson, my coach at Ventura High School (where I attended my first two years of high school) emphasized the bank shot a lot, and the Ventura Youth Basketball League coaches also made us aware of when to use the bank shot. I used it a lot in high school, but I didn't appreciate it as much, particularly the outside bank shot.

The lay-ins, offensive rebound put backs, and turnaround jumpers close to the net all pretty much demand that the backboard is used (unless there is an opportunity to dunk it). But the short jumper from an outside angle is more of a craft that you have to learn and practice. Oddly, although it became an important part of my game at UCLA, I got away from it in the NBA.

The big thing about the bank shot is that there is a greater margin of error. You have to know the angles, you have to practice, and you have to adjust your touch in accordance with the distance from which you are shooting. Sometimes it has to be a soft kiss off the backboard. Sometimes you need a precise pinpoint angle. But in using the backboard properly, the shot is going to fall unless you shoot it much too hard.

Once I incorporated it into my game, it became a big asset to me because I was so thin and quick. I was able to slip through defenses and quickly touch it off the glass. In my all-American years, opposing teams were well aware I averaged double-figure scoring, but they could never figure out how to stop me. My being a thin person made those opponents guarding me think they were superior, even after I'd scored a couple of buckets. I was quicker than they thought, because I knew how to use my body to slither through defenses to take whatever they gave me. The bank shot was a Bruin trademark of every player under Coach Wooden, and with the proficiency I developed, I could bank the correct trajectory off the glass quickly with just the right touch.

Although I became a good ball handler with my left hand, the only shot I took with my left was the hook shot or the easy layup. With the bank shot, I was better able to use my left in traffic. That, in turn, increased my offensive game to not only take what the defense was giving me, but I had mastery over my opponent, because he would have no idea of which direction I would go or when I would get the shot off.

Another asset to my game was that I would try to play my game without trying to show up my opponent or draw attention from the crowd or other players. It was kind of like a little secret that let the opponent know, "You just got beat." As long as I kept it a secret, I could do it again and again. Often I'd score half a dozen buckets before the opposing coach noticed and switched defenders or tried something else.

Being able to can a jumper, go right or left to the bucket, pull up to hit the bank shot, or pass to the open man are key fundamentals of successful individual players and most successful teams. When those skills are put together in a team concept, it lessens the need for excessive ball handling. Every player there had crossover, behind the back, or onside dribble moves, but at UCLA, simplicity and efficiency had a greater value, and the other skills were not well appreciated. Admittedly, with our size, athleticism, quickness, and passing and scoring abilities, we were built to move the ball in the air. There are some programs built to better utilize ball-handling skills.

As freshmen, we didn't come into much contact with Coach Wooden. The March Madness fervor was nothing like it is today. College basketball coaches didn't focus as much on winning an NCAA Championship or getting to the Final Four as they did on beating the UCLA Bruins. There was one thought: beat UCLA. If you can beat UCLA, the NCAA title is yours. *If you can beat UCLA!*

Coach Wooden, however, did stop by to watch our practices from time to time. I could see that he was studying my unorthodox jump shot. I could feel he had some thoughts about suggesting a change. But he and the coaching staff came to the conclusion that, as long as I consistently made the shot and had a good backspin on the ball, they could live with the way I shot the jumper and free throws.

As noted earlier, UCLA practices were very well organized. Time at practice was used very efficiently. With six high-school all-Americans, practices were very competitive, but yet, in the Wooden system, they were very repetitious.

Along with me, Gary Franklin and Vince Carson were freshmen forwards.

Vince was six-seven and had a strong inside game. He was awesome at posting up.

Gary was six-five and had an outside game, but he could also go baseline very well and had good moves around the basket.

I was six-six and fell somewhere between the two. I certainly didn't have the inside game like Vince, and I was not the outside threat that Gary was. I could, however, handle the ball as well or better than either of them.

All the guys on the team respected one another, and we knew why we were there. We were always looking for that competitive edge. In Bill's case, it was obvious he was going to be *the man*, if for no other reason than because he was the only center. Being very talented and practicing with the varsity, he was already on an accelerated pace.

Everyone had a positive attitude about making the varsity when the time would come, and the competition at practices helped us to develop the level of intensity commonly associated with Bruin teams.

As forwards, Vince, Gary, and I knew that once we reached the varsity level, we had to challenge and compete with Larry Farmer, Larry Hollyfield, and John Chapman, who were already in the front-court rotation behind Sidney Wicks, Curtis Rowe, and Steve Patterson. No pressure. These were the support guys helping to lead UCLA to a 29–1 season and another Pac-10 and NCAA championship! After outstanding careers at UCLA, the key guys, Wicks and Rowe, would be moving on to the NBA level. We knew that challenging Hollyfield, Farmer, and Chapman would be an uphill battle. After all, they were going to have the opportunity to have something to say about it.

But with the repetitious and competitive practices at UCLA, our confidence levels kept rising. The upper-classmen may have been future all-American candidates, but there was no shame in our game, and they knew it.

After books and basketball came the young ladies. There were nice-looking, intelligent young ladies, with an incredible assortment of nationalities and sound perspectives on life in general, all around UCLA. Watching young ladies at UCLA is like watching a tennis match, where you're constantly jerking your head from left to right and back again. The Beach Boys hit the nail on the head when they produced the song "California Girls." I'm certain the University of Miami, Michigan, Howard, Texas, and other great institutions of higher learning have their share of dazzling coeds, but to a red-blooded freshman, the coeds made the scenery at UCLA a lot more beautiful. I would hope this forthrightness isn't sexist, but I would be remiss if I failed to point out one of the finer attributes of UCLA to a young fellow.

With the tremendous popularity of UCLA basketball, the freshmen guys got a good share of attention. There were so many wonderful coeds, we joked about the varsity having too many girls and that we would love to get the overspill.

But that was all locker-room jock talk to ease away from the hard competition we handed each other on a daily basis. With all of my adjustments to UCLA and the additional competition I was facing in classes and on the basketball court, I relished my privacy. In actuality, I knew that the girls would always be there.

I got through my freshman year with flying colors, academically and on the basketball court.

I led the freshman team in scoring, and my outside shot improved tremendously. I was not the long-range shooter I was to become in the NBA, but I was very accurate from midrange, and I had perfected the technique of utilizing the bank shot—as all UCLA players were expected to do.

Meanwhile, Curtis, Sidney, Steve Patterson, and Henry Bibby were leading UCLA to Coach Wooden's fifth straight NCAA championship. They went 29–1, losing only to Notre Dame in a game where Austin Carr went wild, scoring forty-six points. Carr was the second leading scorer in the nation that year, averaging thirty-eight points a game. Johnny Neumann of Mississippi was first, with a 40.1 average.

In some circles, it was thought that Coach Wooden didn't mind the loss because the team had gotten complacent and felt that a well-timed loss could be used to his advantage to reign in the attention of the players.

Coach Wooden always stressed consistent intensity. In UCLA game films, you see him looking very calm on the sideline, and he usually was. He basically only worried when complacency seemed to be settling in among the players. Complacency could lead to guys putting forth *less than their best*. His only reaction to the Notre Dame 1971 loss was that it was not as important as a Pac-10 conference loss.

Sidney and Curtis were named all-Americans and were both drafted into the NBA in the first round.

Steve Patterson was named to the NCAA Final Four All-Tournament Team. He was also drafted into the NBA and had a great career. Steve is often referred to as the answer to the trivia question of who played center at UCLA between Kareem Abdul-Jabbar and Bill Walton. The irony is that, as the starting center, Steve won the same amount of NCAA championships as Bill (two) and only one less than Kareem.

UCLA defeated Villanova 68–62 for the title. Steve had twenty-nine points. Howard Porter led Villanova with twenty-five points.

In the semifinal game, Villanova squeaked by a very talented Western Kentucky team in double overtime by a score of 92–89. UCLA had beaten Kansas 68–60 to get to the championship match.

Henry had an unbelievable tournament, shooting seventeen for seventeen in free throws. In the Final Four, he scored eighteen points in the semifinal against Kansas and seventeen in the championship game against the Villanova Wildcats.

Frankly, UCLA barely got out of the Western Regional with a win over Long Beach State and Coach Jerry Tarkanian by a score of 57–55 after trailing 31–27 at halftime. Coach Tarkanian was on the rise of becoming one of the most colorful and winningest coaches in NCAA basketball at Long Beach, UNLV, and Fresno State. His Long Beach team featured two serious ballers in Ed Ratleff and George Trapp.

The UCLA–Long Beach State game was a long-anticipated showdown in the Southern California area between two of the top teams in the nation. Sports fans tend to get excited about the underdog, and in Southern California, Long Beach State had stirred quite a bit of excitement with its up-tempo game and national ranking. But in the end, and at the end of the Regionals, UCLA—with Wicks, Rowe, Patterson, Bibby, Kenny Booker, Terry Schofield, and company—was off to the Final Four, where they met up with fourth-ranked Kansas in the semifinals, winning 68–60.

The Villanova-UCLA matchup was your typical East Coast strong physical game versus the finesse of the West Coast, and Porter was the real deal. Porter was named to the all-tournament team, along with Wicks and Patterson, Jim McDaniel of Western Kentucky, and Hank Siemiontkowski of Villanova.

The UCLA basketball legacy was now at its height – five consecutive NCAA championships and seven total in eight years. The UCLA program was now the class of college basketball, with many players moving on to become stars in the NBA. Kareem was on his way to winning his first NBA championship with Oscar Robertson at Milwaukee, and then there were other veteran NBA names like Gail Goodrich, Keith Erickson, Lynn Shackleford, and Lucius Allen, all UCLA alums. On the way to join them in the NBA were Wicks, Rowe, and Patterson.

One of the things that impressed me was that, during that five-consecutive-championships period, there were only five losses. Also during that period, UCLA only lost three PAC-10 conference games—one in 1969 and two in 1970.

The current overall win streak stood at fifteen games. Little did our freshmen group know that we would continue the streak to a phenomenal *eighty-eight straight.*

Rev. Leo Leander and Mrs. Thelma Wilkes are shown relaxing at home with children (L-R) Jamaal, Naomi, Gail and Leo.

II

PARENTAL GUIDANCE — THE FOUNDATION OF PERSONAL DEVELOPMENT

It was Mom who made it very clear to me that there would be no sports in my life if my school grades were not what she knew I was capable of producing. This was not a negotiable matter with her, and in no way was she going to relax her principles to allow a lesser effort to prevail.

We often remember the exact point of impact when we get our inspiration. For my basketball inspiration, it was watching my sister Naomi. In fact, it was a long-range jumper that hit nothing but net...and then her speedy retrieval of the ball. A cat-quick turnaround and she artfully pumped a midrange jumper—swish! It was poetry in motion. A little work on the dribble drive capped off by a picture-perfect layup with a soft touch off the backboard. Some free throws and then the warm-ups were over. She was ready to take on the guys in a full-court game.

Watching her hold her own against some of the best teenage, playground hoopsters was one of my favorite pastimes as a kid. She was very inspirational to me, as were a number of other varsity high-school basketball players in the Ventura–Oxnard–Santa Barbara area.

Naomi had it all. She was a great athlete. Had women's basketball been as popular as it is today, she definitely would have been one of the big names in NCAA women's basketball, the WNBA, and, in my shamelessly biased opinion, a member of the Naismith Basketball Hall of Fame. She could handle the ball, move, and score. She couldn't be intimidated. But she could intimidate. Her skills did the talking. I was more interested in baseball in my earlier years, but her skills on the court formed a blueprint for Jamaal Keith Wilkes the basketball player.

Naomi was also a brilliant student who would go on to earn a law degree from the University of Southern California. She earned her undergraduate degree at Stanford University. One of her career highlights was becoming the first woman to successfully negotiate a contract for a top-level professional athlete. Mine.

My sister Gail, also an excellent student, attended the University of San Francisco. Together, the girls put a lot of pressure on my brother, Leo, and me to do well in school. Just wanting to measure up to their levels was my basic goals in those years.

As I've said, we never know from where our inspiration comes at its first point of impact. Little was I to know that idolizing my sister playing basketball was to propel me to an athletic career that included an opportunity to play under the late, great John Wooden, one of the finest men God put on this earth, and the greatest basketball coach in history. It was a career that would also include being a part of two NCAA titles at UCLA, four National Basketball Association titles as a professional, and election to the Hall of Fame as part of the class of 2012.

In all, I had a career spanning eighteen years, from high school to the professional ranks, playing on six championship teams (not including conference and divisional championships), ten championship final games or final series, and playing on a play-off team in every year in which I played a full season in organized sports. The only year I did not make the play-offs was my injury-shortened season with the Los Angles Clippers, my final professional year.

I have been blessed to have had extraordinary people guiding me, beginning with my parents, my sisters Gail and Naomi, my brother, Leo, and my favorite coaches John Wooden and Bob Swanson of Ventura High School.

There also were a couple of older guys whose high-quality character captured my admiration. One was Virgil Roberts, an older guy from my high school who went on to attend UCLA and Harvard Law School. The other was David Lawyer, an exceptional student athlete at Oxnard High School, whom I admired when I was a fledgling hoopster in the Ventura Youth Basketball Association. David went on to attend Princeton University.

My parents were fairly prominent people in the Ventura area, largely because my dad, the late Reverend

Leo Leander Wilkes, was a pastor at Olivet Baptist Church.
My mother, Thelma Naomi (Benson) Wilkes, was an
administrator with the State of California Employment
Development Department. Both were born to parents
who had dual roles of being farmers and educators in
the Arkansas. My paternal grandparents also owned a
mom-and-pop grocery store.

While living in Arkansas, Dad was a real good semipro
baseball player as an infielder and pitcher. He caught the
attention of a couple of Negro League scouts but opted
for marriage and family life.

It was in Dayton, Ohio, where I started kindergarten.
Although I actually was born in Berkeley, California, and
spent the majority of my life in Southern California, I do
have some fond memories of life in the Midwest, such as
throwing snowballs and going on sleigh rides.

Dayton, Ohio, is where I got my first pair of sneakers.
They were PF Flyers. I had seen them advertised on
television, and some of the kids wore them. When Dad
bought a pair for me, I was so ecstatic that I just ran all
day long, up and down the street like a bronco stallion
trying to gain the attention of a filly. I had no particular
destination. No purpose. It was just uncontrollable
energy and happiness. As a professional basketball
player, I promoted a couple of brand-name basketball
shoes, but my heart belongs to PF Flyers.

Dad was a well-read man and very knowledgeable—
far beyond theology, the art of preaching, and being
able to recite scripture at the drop of a hat. He contin-
uously imparted words of wisdom that made you stop

and appreciate the importance of character-building concerns, such as morality, self-actualization, ethnic values, academic achievement, and people skills.

Before the widespread interest of African American history and black social consciousness, Dad taught us about ancient African civilizations, such as Songhay and Timbuktu, and great kings of African countries, such as Askia Muhammad, Hannibal, and Shaka. He told us of the many great accomplishments of Americans of African descent. Among them were civil engineer Benjamin Banneker, historian and educator Dr. Carter G. Woodson, and airplane inventor James Smith. When he spoke of inventors, he always had or was able to quickly produce documentation of patent numbers and dates to prove the authenticity of their inventions, even though others in American history may have received the public credit.

Dad pointed out that many inventions that have proven to be essential to the economy of this nation came from the minds of people of African descent, such as the horseshoe and the cotton chopper.

His purpose was to create a sense of appreciation of our country and illustrate that each ethnic group in America, including African Americans, made important contributions. He raised us to be men and women first and to appreciate our ethnicity second.

As a man of faith and one whose life was dedicated to inspiring, counseling, and healing others, Dad was a man uniquely rich with precious stones of profound wisdom, and he was clever and methodically deft at imparting reflections and insights very proficiently. In fact, he was so adept that there often were times when he would not say anything but offer an attentive pastoral expression of approval, or a gesture that would suggest that something you just said or did perhaps could have been handled in a better manner or, conversely, was well handled.

Some of the values he taught us, that I still hold strongly, are that one should always be in control of his or her thoughts; that one should always be in control of his or her actions; to hold steadfast to your sense of purpose; to not be resentful when treated wrongly; and the importance of having the confidence in the ability of your teacher to teach you.

He emphasized the power of concentration and that we should, at all times, be in control of ourselves and not influenced by others. This is particularly helpful in one's young-adult years when we are all vulnerable to outside influences that may be socially and personally detrimental.

He also stressed that we ought to not get hung up in resenting people regardless of what they do to us because such resentment and negative reaction only serves to retard our own personal development.

Early on, I learned from Dad that, if a pupil does not have a high regard for his or her teacher, it is perhaps his or her greatest handicap. As a result, I never had problems with school and was able to maximize my educational experiences. This also proved to be immensely important in my basketball development, with specific regard to my initial meetings with Coach Swanson.

While playing playground basketball with my buddies, Coach Swanson would stop to watch us. He was head basketball coach at Ventura High School and an easily recognizable local celebrity well known to each of us.

Coach Swanson would take a moment, from time to time, to explain a couple of skills that he kindly suggested I should consider working on to improve my game. This went on for a few years before we had a formal friendship.

This all was very flattering to me, to receive fundamental basketball counseling from the Ventura basketball guru. Plus, he was so super nice and very clear on making his points. Even though his comments were informal and suggestive only, I took them seriously and worked hard.

In the rearing of my sisters, Leo, and I, Dad's bottom line was that—if we would apply self-control, not harbor resentment, and have confidence in the ability of those teaching or trying to help us—our belief system and moral values would be pretty sound.

Mom's big thing was that we shouldn't settle for less than we were capable of achieving. It was something that Dad also stressed, but performing less than what you were capable of doing is one thing Mom would react to with lightening speed and quickly sit you down until it was clear in your head.

It was Mom who made it very clear to me that there would be no sports in my life if my school grades were not what she knew I was capable of producing. This was not a negotiable matter with her, and in no way was she going to relax her principles to allow a lesser effort to prevail.

There was one particular occasion that was pretty much a turning point in my understanding about balancing school and sports. This emanated from that tell-all document we know well as the *report card*. I received a progress report during my seventh-grade year that had four As and three Cs. Since some of my buddies, new friends in junior high school, had Ds and Fs, I thought that my report card was excellent. And in comparison, it was. I soon was to learn that such thinking was my first mistake, and comparing my progress report to the abilities of others and not my own abilities was a remedy for a life lesson.

I went home thinking I had done well. I gave Mom my report card, changed clothes, and was on my way back out the door to play basketball. Mom stopped me. "Sit

Elementary School Jamaal (Jackson) Keith Wilkes

down, Sonny." (Sonny is my family nickname.) Calmly, with an endearing inquisitive expression, she asked, "Do you like playing basketball?"

"Of course I do," I responded.

Then she turned on the heat.

Her usual sweet and gentle voice jumped two decibels, and her tone shifted gears from a motherly pleasantry to what seemed to me to be life-threatening.

"Did you hear me? If you want to play basketball, you are going to have to do better," she demanded. Clearly, this was not a threat; it was a promise.

I was dumfounded and scared. Had they had a child-abuse hotline then, I would have called. Instead, there was an immediate majestic growth—an epiphany—in my understanding of what was expected of me at home and that I ought to expect more of myself.

I was scared into reality by her threatening—her promising—to remove basketball from my life. I became embarrassed. She was so very right. I had performed less than I was capable of doing. But I first had to sort through my thinking that, in comparison to other students, I was bringing in a good report card. Although her mandate was clear and had a bone-chilling effect that pushed me to do well in school in order to keep my basketball playing privileges, it wasn't until years later that I fully appreciated what she had done for me.

I became determined to never have that same conversation again—with my mother or anyone else. There would never again be a progress report that didn't show progress. Just the idea that I might never again play basketball was enough to kick things into proper perspective. I knew full well that she was as serious as the heat of fire.

In regard to underachieving, Dad's philosophical way of putting it was that it was not wise to reach for the lower end of things when the higher things of life are given. If an individual is capable of performing at one level, then it was a sin to settle for less.

The social values and spiritual enlightenment that my sisters, brother, and I received at home served as a strong foundation for positive socialization experiences that were to come later through church, youth organizations, high school, and higher education.

Our rearing was rooted in our parents' love for us, and we reciprocated with a strong sense of obedience and honesty.

Like Dad, I firmly believe that obedience is essential to proper development, and young people have a duty to obey, regardless of whether parents are right tr wrong (in a general philosophical sense).

Each American household has its challenges and certain advantages or disadvantages, and while some may be far too complicated to address here, in general, there is absolutely no excuse for young people not obeying their parents and guardians.

Many of the problems associated with young people can be directly traced to lack of obedience or parental guidance. Parents must put in double time, triple time, and maybe even overtime (whatever it takes) to develop appropriate rapport to establish obedience. Obedience doesn't have to be about confrontation or negativity. It could just as easily, and perhaps with more impact, stem from positive interaction.

Honesty is something that also was imperative in our household. There are countless external influences, many of which are negative and can lead one into trouble. Whatever trouble situation in which we may find ourselves, being honest with our parents is like a bridge over troubled waters and our best bet to correct the situation.

Learning the game under early tutelage of Coach Bob Swanson, who at that time was varsity basketball coach at Ventura High School.

III

EARLY YEARS IN ORGANIZED SPORTS

I was eight years old when I first came into contact with Coach Bob Swanson, the Ventura High School basketball coach. One day during a break between playground basketball games, he came over and said to me, "Say, son, you're pretty good." Then he asked the question that became my first major piece of advice in basketball: "Can you use your left hand to dribble?"

My first organized sport was baseball. Even today, I am very fond of baseball. I started playing when I was seven years old, and it was instant romance. I later began playing in a winter weekend basketball league at age nine, but by far, I liked baseball more.

I was a do-everything Little Leaguer: the outfield, the infield, or pitching. My dad really got into it with me and taught me the different pitches, fielding and hitting, and even the psychology of the game. He spent a lot of time pitching batting practice to Leo and me.

I used to have quite a bad temper at that age, so Dad had to talk to me a lot.

"Look, Sonny," he would begin, "whatever you do, never lose your cue."

What he meant was that I shouldn't get upset at something like a questionable call by the umpire or an error by a teammate, because it could throw off my whole game.

"Don't defeat yourself," he stressed.

I've never been anything close to a violent person, but my temper during my early years was something my sisters and brother didn't want to see. My sister Gail says my face would swell and that you could see my blood boil. She said it was a real devil look, a look as though I really felt ill will toward something or somebody. She says I was always willing to listen, up to a point. Beyond that point, those who knew me well knew to back off.

My mother never saw my temperamental side, thank goodness. Fortunately, it was a personality trait my dad straightened out early on.

My birth name is Jackson Keith Wilkes. Since all the kids knew me in school as Jackson Wilkes, they called me Jackie during my first year in Little League. Jackie Robinson was still an exciting name in baseball, although his playing career had ended. They called me Jackie, in part, to associate me with him and our team with his level of performance. It was quite flattering, and I played enthusiastically and with pride, but I've been partial to my middle name, Keith.

I used a black baseball glove, which was made in Japan. In sports, guys will find humor in any little thing about you. With me, it was the glove. It was not one of the designer American gloves with an autograph by Mickey Mantle or Don Drysdale, but it suited me just fine. Nevertheless, some of the guys would laugh and make fun of the glove. The wisecracks were impersonal and were funny and creative; I even chuckled. It was all in good clean fun. The irony is that, today when you hear of something made in Japan, it signals top quality, and you have to get in line to buy it.

I also had a speech impediment, and I stuttered quite badly. It was so bad that it affected my classroom participation at school. I was afraid to try to answer a question in class because, seemingly, it took about three minutes for me to release the first syllable. But in my second-grade year, I had a speech-therapy class with my best friend Wilfred Brown.

Wilfred and I made quite a pair. He was short and chubby, and I was tall and skinny. We both stuttered something awful. Thanks to the therapy class, we were able to get control of the stuttering. I'm glad to have had a friend like Wilfred to team up with to overcome the problem. On occasion, it takes me a few seconds still to get into the flow of a sentence when I'm very tired.

I had great support when I attended grade school in Ventura. My mother was very active with the Parent-Teacher Association. My second-grade teacher was Ms. Mesa, who was a wonderful lady, and I remember her well.

Of course, having two sisters ahead of me who excelled in school put a lot of pressure on me to do well. Additionally, as a black family in a predominately white community like Ventura, we were highly motivated to be known as a successful family unit.

It wasn't long before other teachers would have me involved with helping other kids in third grade. That activity carried over into my fourth-grade year with Miss Odor, who had a fourth-and-fifth-grade combination class. I was soon doing fifth-grade-level work and at the end of the year. I received a double promotion to sixth grade.

Academically, the double promotion had no impact. Athletically, it had no impact. But it was frustrating for me in my music class. I was learning to play the clarinet and saxophone, and skipping a year was too difficult to handle.

Socially, moving up two grades was not a major issue since I was often around older kids. However, skipping a grade did put me a notch away from the daily group of friends I had been with since second grade.

In addition to balancing schoolwork with basketball in the winter and baseball in the spring, I was very active in church. Church was a huge part of my life. Leo and I sang in the Sunshine Youth Choir. The choir performed at other churches, as well as ours. Leo and I were featured on duets. In fact, on many occasions, just the two of us appeared to sing duets at other churches. Being a part of bringing about good spiritual feelings to people was a great experience in my life.

I also was a Sunday school leader (and later taught Sunday school class), and I served on the junior usher board. Although being a preacher's son obviously impacted my enthusiasm and extensive degree of activity in the church, I thoroughly enjoyed and looked forward to everything in which I was involved.

I know of others who didn't handle being the son or daughter of a preacher too well. There is social pressure, and like all pressure, it can have either a positive or negative impact. For the most part, the preacher's kid becomes one who excels and serves as a role model to other youths.

While our home environment was fairly subdued and serious, it was a very happy household, and one free of complications. Among us kids, we were each other's best friends. My parents were only really strict in two areas: study habits for one, and if we left the house together, it was imperative that we returned together. As long as we did well in school and obeyed, we could have all the privileges there were to be had.

I was eight years old when I first came into contact with Coach Bob Swanson, the Ventura High School head basketball coach. As I noted earlier, he kept an eye on the playgrounds and had seen me playing.

One day during a break between games, he came over to me and said, "Say, son, you're pretty good." Then he asked a question that became my first major piece of advice in basketball: "Can you use your left hand to dribble?"

I never had thought about using my left!

In fact, I didn't really think at all on the basketball court at that age. I just outran everybody up and down the court and shot the ball up to the hoop.

Mr. Swanson's comment started me thinking about what I was doing on the court. In a very soft-spoken, nonchalant way, he really got my attention. Ventura was and still is a big basketball town, and the man who was speaking to me was one of the biggest people in town. He was bigger than the mayor. Hardly anyone on the playground, including myself, knew who the mayor was. *I still don't know.* Everybody knew who Bob Swanson was.

"My left hand? Only a little, sir. I really never think about it," I responded.

"Well then," he said, "let me tell you about this league you might be interested in."

My attention was keyed on his every word. He went on to tell me about the Ventura Youth Basketball Association (VYBA), which would be having tryouts a few months later. He assured me I would learn how to use my left hand and that he hoped he would see me there.

Everyone made a team and got to play at least one quarter. With my height and athletic ability, I became a starter. The VYBA turned out to be a very good program with great organization, and all the kids—regardless of ability—got to play.

For the next several years, it was basically Little League baseball in the spring and summer, flag football in the fall, and VYBA basketball in the winter. Although my basketball team finished in first place just about every year, I didn't pay much attention to my basketball skills because I was engulfed with wanting to succeed in baseball.

I continued to run into Coach Swanson, who, more and more, would continue to suggest some basketball skills I should try to develop. We had no formal relationship, but because of my upbringing and recognition of who he was, I always gave him the utmost respect right from the start. Whatever he suggested or even hinted at, I immediately began working hard at it.

The turning point at which basketball emerged as my principal sport of concentration didn't occur until the year before I went into senior high school.

Coach Swanson approached me at the outset of that summer. "I think you're quite a talent," he said. "Some people think you can help the varsity right away. I'm one of them.

"But of course, there are others who are not convinced. If this is something you really want to try for, it might be wise to play with some of my returning players this summer and lift some weights."

Ventura was a big basketball town. At the heart of it all were the high-school and junior-college teams. If you were to ask people in Ventura about which team they had the most interest in—even in comparison to the Dodgers, Los Angeles Rams, Lakers, USC Trojans, or UCLA Bruins—they quickly would say Ventura High School basketball. Up the road a bit in our neighboring town of Santa Barbara, the big fan interest was in football.

So for a youngster who's been successful in youth basketball and thinking that he can play a little hoop, the idea of being on the Ventura High School varsity basketball team was exciting. With basketball being such as it was in Ventura, the high school program was loaded with talent, and passing over junior-varsity teams meant that I was just about ready for prime time.

Ever since my double promotion from fourth to sixth grade, I had been competing with older kids in every way—academically and athletically. I was quite thin, which was cause for locker-room jokes. Nevertheless, going up against bigger and stronger athletes was a well-received challenge and an opportunity to show those who questioned my thin frame that I could not only handle myself but excel.

The challenges about my size turned out to be just the beginning. I would have to overcome them again and again, and, in fact, I never put them to rest until I was a veteran in the National Basketball Association. Even then, when I had to go into the paint against guys like Darryl Dawkins, Elvin Hayes, Moses Malone, Maurice Lucas, Wes Unseld, and Bob Lanier, the average person wouldn't put up a wooden nickel for my chances. The record, of course, now shows four NBA championships and a Hall of Fame career.

Actually, the biggest concern I had in stepping up to Coach Swanson's challenge was that it presented a major dilemma in having to make a decision between giving up my last year of Babe Ruth League baseball to concentrate on basketball. I never had to choose between the two before. The basketball tradition in the city was dominant. Overwhelming, in fact. I began to look at basketball as something that could lead to more. I decided to go for it.

Prior to high school, I played at Cabrillo Junior High School under Coach George Petersen, in addition to my team in the VYBA. It was a period in my life in which I experienced some physically difficult growing pains. My bones were growing faster than the rest of my body, and because of the pain, I could only do so much running. The doctors clearly described the problem as Osgood's

Schlatter, a temporary condition that affects kids during their growth spurts and wreaks havoc with tall people and athletes in particular. They prepared me psychologically for the discomfort I would have to go through. With the doctor's reassurance, I got through it OK.

At Cabrillo, we finished second to Anacapa, which had Roger at center. Roger was a great competitor and would be a competitive nemesis for me throughout the next few years. Anacapa had beaten us by five points. I was very disappointed. My competitive spirit in basketball was beginning to manifest itself.

I also had been playing pickup basketball at the Westside Boys Club (now the Boys and Girls Club) in Ventura. I also played in pickup games at Ventura High School. In most games there, I played older guys. The Boys Club is where I learned to make adjustments to compensate for my size disadvantages when playing against older, taller, and stronger guys.

It was at the Boys Club that I learned to interact with people.

I got into a shoving match with this new kid from Germany named Dale Schumpert. He had a distinctive German accent. It was my first person-to-person encounter with someone just learning the English language. Unexposed to international diversity at my rather young age, I though this German accent was strange—funny, in fact. I thought he was from another planet. Of course, when he laid eyes on me, a very tall, black, skinny kid, he probably thought the same.

During arts and crafts, we both wanted the same material at the same time and became embroiled in a disagreement. Unable to communicate, we did the next best thing; we began pushing and shoving, and our arms were flailing at each other.

Just as quickly as the shoving started, it ended. We became friends and frequently hung out at each other's homes.

The Westside Boys Club was a great place for me to interact on a noncompetitive basis. It seemed like, at school and in sports, my activities were competitive, and the club was a welcome change of scenery. But the Schumpert incident was the first of several people skills the Boys Club helped me develop.

To this day, I have had the Boys Club and Girls of America at heart and have served as a national spokesperson for them. I have benefited from and truly believe in the saying: The Boys and Girls Clubs of America are clubs that beat the streets. Instead of spending my downtime in the streets, I just went to the Boys Club and played pickup basketball.

Although basketball had been second fiddle to baseball, I, by now, had become a fairly accomplished young basketball player for my age group. In addition to having the main ingredient of height, I had skills.

As I headed into senior high school, it was bye-bye baseball, hello hoop ball.

I always had kept myself abreast of the community sports news and information about high-school basketball in Ventura and surrounding areas. There were some real good players that I enjoyed reading about and getting to know: Rex Kochel, a one-eyed, six-four forward; Booker T. Gilford, a slick, six-five stud; Marty Litchcote, a six-five forward who went on to play college ball in Utah; and Joe Christman, a forward who went to UCLA and played with Kareem Abdul-Jabbar (Lew Alcindor), Lucius Allen, Mike Warren, and Lynn Shackelford. The star of the team during my first year was Danny Roberts. Since I had relatives and friends in nearby Santa Barbara, I also kept abreast of their players. The guys I followed mostly were David Varner and the Lambert brothers, Chris and Wiggins.

Danny was the one of the older guys my sister Naomi played with and against in pickup games on the playground. He was one of four Roberts brothers. Danny's older brother, Virgil, who went on to earn a law degree at Harvard University, was a great role model for me. He was a very intelligent and well-rounded student. My classmate in the Roberts family was Duane, with whom I played baseball and basketball. Behind was the fourth Roberts brother, Chris.

My idol at the high-school level was David Lawyer, a six-five forward who played at Oxnard High School, our number one rival.

In a competitive sense, I hated the Oxnard Yellowjackets. But I thought David Lawyer was the best basketball player in the world. Like Virgil Roberts, David had it all. He was an intelligent, charismatic student who was involved in all the right things and became a basketball legend before going on to Princeton. I kept up with his progress and nearly followed in his footsteps to the prestigious Ivy League.

I gained a lot from being exposed to and knowing Virgil, whose excellence and achievements throughout his life have been admirable, but it was David who I patterned myself after most as a student athlete.

At the pro level, my biggest idol was Elgin Baylor. His younger brother John Baylor attended our church and became our associate pastor. He also was one of my Sunday school teachers. Mr. Baylor once arranged for me to go to one of Elgin's basketball camps. He took my mom and me to a Laker game where we met Elgin afterward.

I remember seeing Wilt Chamberlain in person for the first time that same night. He was dressed in a cold-blooded black suit with a black shirt, a black tie, and a black derby hat. I had never seen anybody dress that sophisticated, not to mention a seven-foot person. At the time I was five-nine and eleven years old.

I was slightly aware of the question of whether I would be able to contribute to the Ventura High School varsity team as a sophomore. Naturally, there were doubts. But it was possible. Coach Swanson's remarks made the possibility an official opportunity for me to seize the moment. I knew, if I focused on it, that it would be something I could achieve.

That summer of 1967, I played a lot of basketball, tightened up some fundamentals, and picked up some additional skills. I learned to play with my back to the basket, which was something I didn't have to concentrate on in youth leagues. In fact, in VYBA, I didn't have to concentrate much on any of those things because I did everything, including handling the ball.

I learned to use both hands well. I learned to shoot hook shots, both right- and left-handed. I learned how to use the glass—something that John Wooden would later underscore big time.

Fortunately for me, Coach Swanson had been orientating me to fundamentals that would enable me to quickly fit into the Ventura High system. Ventura played up-tempo basketball, which was very exciting, very intense fast-break basketball.

Coach Swanson stressed teamwork, ball movement, and intelligent shot selection. All five players on the floor knew where everyone was on the court and, therefore, pretty much knew how opponents would act and react. We would project two or three moves ahead, and for whatever they would do, we already had an answer. You would never find anyone on any Bob Swanson team holding the ball too long or standing around watching the paint dry. If you wanted to be a spectator, you'd have to buy a ticket and sit in the stands, because you could never suit up for Coach Swanson.

Danny Roberts was a senior and the star of the team during my sophomore year. He and Robert Turner were the forwards. Matt Furey was the point guard, and Glen Hannah was the off guard. I had played in the VYBA with Turner and Hannah. It wasn't until a couple of weeks before the season started that Coach Swanson told me that I was the starting center. I was competing very hard against a very talented player named David Myers (not the David Meyers of UCLA and NBA fame).

Like most other athletes who are fortunate enough to go on to play professional sports, I put in long hours.

Hour after hour, I was out there working on my game. At home, we developed a court on hard and brittle dirt in the backyard. It was kind of hard to dribble the ball, but that only helped me learn to handle the ball better.

All of the effort I made never seemed like work. It was fun. And going into high school with an opportunity to start was a big deal.

My first nickname in sports was "Spider" because I was long and gangly. I now stood six-four and weighed 140 pounds. My assets were quickness and getting my shot off.

During our first serious basketball summer, I learned that basketball was a game of space and footwork. Once I had that down and coupled it with my quickness, I was virtually unstoppable. The only players who could give me trouble would be those whose only mission was to stay in my jock and not worry about anything else going on the court or in life. I admit, however, that some of the older, beefy players with experience knew how to lean on me and wear me down, but no one could stop me.

Athletically, I was ready for my first year of varsity basketball. I had the experience and maturity from having played with older guys over several years. Coach Swanson took a lot of pressure off by letting us know that if we won, we deserved the credit but that if we lost, it would be he who would shoulder the responsibility.

We went on to win the Southern California Channel League title with a 12–2 record. Overall, we were 20–7. We lost a heartbreaker in the state play-offs. Aviation High School defeated us 61–60 in the California

Interscholastic Federation (CIF) play-offs. Paul Westphal of USC and NBA fame was the star of the Aviation team.

The Aviation loss was one that shouldn't have been. We were up by one point at 60–59 with the clock running out, and we had possession of the ball. Coach Swanson called time-out and instructed us, "No matter what, don't shoot the ball!"

What followed was an important lesson of which all players, particularly young players, should take note.

Robert Turner was a sharpshooting forward who could fill it up with the best. With the adrenaline flowing, our spirits high, and victory seemingly at hand—which would allow us to move on in the CIF play-offs—Turner put a shot up that he typically makes the greater percentage of the time. This time it was not to be. As the shot descended from its arch, it appeared headed into the basket cylinder. Then all of a sudden, it caught the back of the rim and rammed back out, and Aviation rebounded.

Aviation called time-out with four seconds on the clock. When play resumed, we were all down in spirits. Westphal caught us sleeping and worked himself loose under the basket to receive a half-court pass and score a game-winning layup.

As it is said in the Rudyard Kipling poem "If" ("If you can keep your head, when all about you is insane..."), so it was with Coach Swanson. While Aviation's team and fans were going absolutely berserk, and as we were stunned, Coach Swanson kept his head and was the epitome of a class act. We had the game won and lost it. He recognized that we were teenagers who sometimes make mistakes, but we were also people with pride and emotions.

Turner was more stunned than any of us. Each of us on the team, our fans, and anybody familiar with the team knew that eight out of ten times he makes the shot. There were several games he busted open for us or was counted upon to score from a play designed with him as a first option in a crucial moment. This one he missed by a centimeter. He was a prolific shooter who had a wide-open shot and excellent opportunity to ice the game.

We didn't quite know how to react to everything. Turner was a team leader and one of the most popular guys on the team and throughout school. He took a shot that any of us might have taken given the same set of circumstances. Like most teenagers, and despite Coach Swanson's specific instructions, we didn't see Turner's decisions as something wrong. But as a team, we did feel that we had let Coach Swanson down. We came to understand clearly, through that experience, that the coach decides what's best for the team.

Compton High School won the CIF Championship that year. Compton was led by my future UCLA teammate Larry Hollyfield. Compton was awesome, dominating Southern California in the late 1960s. Hollyfield was one of the best prep athletes in California high-school history. At Compton High School, one year at Compton College, and three years at UCLA, he never lost a basketball game that he started. *Never*. He was a three-sport star (football, basketball, and baseball) and nearly became the first to win CIF Player of the Year in two sports (basketball and baseball). He won the basketball honor but narrowly lost the baseball honor to Jeff Burroughs, who went on to have an outstanding Major League Baseball career.

But we had our own big star in Danny Roberts. In addition to winning the Channel League MVP Award, Danny broke the school record of career points. The previous record was 954. Danny shattered the mark with 1,188 points during his three years.

For me, the best thing during the season was beating our biggest rival, the Oxnard Yellowjackets. We also registered another big victory against my individual rival, Roger Perry, who played for crosstown rival Buena High School.

It was an exciting season with tremendous personal growth for me. Playing before a large crowd every game was an unforgettable experience and certainly prepared me for what was to come, not just the following year, but for the next fifteen.

VENTURA HIGH STARTERS - Keith Wilkes, Glen Hannah, Matt
Fury, Coach Swanson, Danny Roberts, and Robert Turner

IV

EMERGING AS A BASKETBALL CELEBRITY

An invitation or encouragement to participate in a wrongdoing, such as drugs, doesn't mean that you will not be socially accepted if you don't do the wrong. After turning down invitations a few times, people will get the message that you are no one who fools around with drugs. You don't have to make a big issue of it, or have some excuse, or apologize; just say, "No thanks."

After my varsity season, I became a lightweight celebrity. Can you imagine such a thing, Spider the celeb?

It started changing my life, and, truthfully, I was eating it up. I was very comfortable with being known all over town. It was the first real big-time recognition I received as a result of playing basketball.

The year was 1968. In addition to the emergence of my coming of age in basketball, there was another coming-of-age phenomenon. It was social consciousness. The civil rights movement was at its peak, and on its heels came the era of the black-power and peace movements. It was an era of cultural and sexual revolutions. The civil rights movement sparked hope in everyone, not just those wanting voting rights or integration, but everyone: blacks, women, Hispanics, hippies, draft dodgers, and anyone who felt *the system* was keeping them down.

"We shall overcome" was giving way to "black power, my brother." "As-salaam alaikum." "More power to the people." "Peace, brother, and peace, sister." "Hell no, we won't go!" "Gay pride." Those were the emerging religious, cultural, and social revolution battle cries across America, and California was leading the charge. California established itself as the most progressive state in advancing social causes for all people. The epicenter was the Bay Area.

Both of my sisters were attending college in the Bay Area at this time. They were amid Haight/Ashbury crowds in the flower-power movement and the fervor of the anti–Vietnam War and peace demonstrations in San Francisco. Across the Bay Bridge was Oakland, the birthplace and home of the Black Panther Party with its leaders Huey P. Newton, Bobby Seales, and Eldridge Cleavor. Political rhetoric abounded. The one thing they all had in common was being anti-establishment. There were names for anyone associated with the establishment: the man, the pig, Uncle Tom, sellout.

Like most, I was deeply affected by the assassinations of Dr. Martin Luther King Jr., who, like my father, was a Baptist preacher, and Bobby Kennedy. Here were two men who clearly stood for and symbolized peace. Their deaths cast a cloud over goodness and righteousness and gave rise to rhetoric. It seemed if the peaceful approach of King and Kennedy to address social ills was not the answer, then maybe Stokely Carmichael and H. Rap Brown had the answer in black power. Maybe Elijah Muhammad had the answer in black separation.

Still yet, there was an emerging message of morality coming out of the Chicano Movement, and farming communities in particular: *Si, se puede* ("Yes, it can be done!"). And who was this Caesar Chavez guy? People started caring about what was going on with South and Central American Latinos, people in the Caribbean countries, people in Asian countries, Native Americans, and people in third-world countries in the Middle East and on the African continent, from Tripoli to Pretoria.

There was a lot more history and sociology than what was presented in high-school classes.

If you were among the rhetoricians, the conversations were endless. There was a growing consciousness in America of the Trail of Tears and the plight of Native Americans; the Palestinian Liberation Organization and strife in the Gaza Strip steeped in biblical history; and the African National Congress (Spear of the Nation) standing up to social and humanitarian atrocities in South Africa.

Meanwhile there were revolutions of another kind across the Pacific, where economic miracles from advancements in industries and technologies created the Four Asian Tigers: Taiwan, South Korea, Hong Kong, and Singapore.

During my preteen years, my family visited another family we knew from Baptist-church circles. The family we visited lived in the Watts section of Los Angeles. It was the day the Watts riot broke out.

I recall hearing a lot of rapid firing, which sounded like a lot of firecrackers going off. I saw people running out of stores with merchandise. I didn't know what was happening at the moment, and I didn't equate it with danger. My mother, however, knew immediately there was imminent danger and got us out of there quickly.

Up in Ventura, about sixty miles northward along the Pacific Coast, people were aware of the Watts riots and related issues that prompted the unrest, but ours was a surfer town. It was an agricultural area with beachfront that made it a very typical California coastal town. It is best characterized, or certainly was then, as being very laid-back. Ventura is pretty much like what you hear about Californians.

Perhaps not as cosmopolitan as Los Angeles, Ventura was diverse, and it was reflected in the airwaves with various kinds of music, from the Beach Boys to Jimmy Hendrix, from the Beatles to Eric Burton and War, and from Taj Mahal to the Temptations. Most of the music reflected social issues. Although Ventura was a laid-back town, through the media and the music, we felt involved with what was going on in Watts and increasingly began to understand more about the world.

Visiting my sisters and their friends in the Bay Area and having continual dialogue with my father, my social consciousness was even further enhanced. In all, this was an era that gave birth to my sense of social awareness. To this day, through changing times and social issues, going from an awakening teenager to being a parent of three adults, I have been mindful of what's going on in and around the world.

In the middle of the society's ball of confusion in the late 1960s, there was basketball, and I was becoming entrenched in the sport and the glory. I was the emerging star of a high-school varsity team in a town where basketball reigned supreme.

With my father being the pastor of a prominent Baptist church, Christ was the center of life in our household and with me personally. I always have reveled in the glory and sanctity of Jesus Christ as my lord and savior to this day. I thank God on a daily basis for all the joys and experiences that life has brought.

Beyond school, church, and basketball, the main delight of my social life was going to see my friend Tony Triguerio and his band perform. Tony was a great bass guitarist who could really get off. His band was similar to Eric Burton and War. I enjoyed them so much that I'd even go to Tony's practice sessions.

There were no real gangs in Ventura. There were a few tough guys who liked to hang out, but not gangs. There was a developing presence of hippies in the Ventura area, but around this time, I was far too focused on basketball and going away to college someday.

Like most young men in their mid teens, I started feeling the spirits of adulthood, mentally and physically. In sports, I had made a quantum leap from a skinny untested kid to a national blue-chip prep basketball star. My awareness of self was growing as fast as my skinny body. The transition years from childhood to young adulthood always has been an interesting phenomenon of life. Not quite as spectacular as birth, of course, but certainly very interesting.

It is a transformation in which we go from total dependency and having no meaningful concerns to a state of mind in which we become self-determined to the extent our parents and those that supervise us will let us get away with.

With my sisters away at college—Gail at the University of San Francisco and Naomi at Stanford—it was only natural to look forward to the day when I would be leaving home for the hallowed halls of higher learning.

While my family was, by no means, poor, neither were we wealthy. I was completely aware that whatever I could do to help myself get to and through college would be vital. Accordingly, my concentration on basketball and academics accelerated.

In my junior year at Ventura High School, I took all the college preparation classes (including Latin) and became active in various extracurricular activities.

It was during my junior year that I was first exposed to drugs.

Since I was so involved with many different activities, I always was rushing from one to the other. One day, I was rushing to the gym for basketball practice.

One of my buddies named Bobby, who was a good friend going way back to Little League days, was sitting around smoking marijuana and drinking wine with some girls. They invited me to join them.

I had heard about grass, but I never had been approached with an invitation to smoke it. Bobby was a good friend and a good, fun-loving guy, but I'm glad I was rushing, because I really never stopped long enough to think about the invitation. His mild invitation turned into an egging kind of thing to get me to join in. I really didn't know anything about grass and, at that moment, couldn't have cared less. I just kept stepping and declined, telling them I had to get to practice. As I moved on, he offered me a parting comment that I didn't hear, there was some laughter, and he yelled to tell me to have a good practice.

There were other times that I was invited to partake in drugs. After all, this was the sixties. With the prevalence of drugs came the saying, "If you can remember the sixties, you weren't there." No has always been the answer. I always was firm but never condemned those who were into drugs. Taking that approach enabled me to socialize with everybody.

Peer pressure has been around since the beginning of time, and I understand its influence on young people. I think that if young people really think twice, peer pressure is largely self-inflicted.

An invitation or encouragement to participate in a wrongdoing, such as drugs, doesn't mean you will not be socially accepted if you don't do the wrong. After turning down invitations a few times, people will get the message that you are not one who fools around with drugs. Most importantly, they will know that, when you say "no," what you really mean is "no." You don't have to make a big issue of it, have some excuse, or apologize; just say, "No thanks."

As far as basketball was concerned, I had a personal goal in my junior year. My goal was to be a leader.

With Danny Roberts having graduated, the team would need a leader. You might say I was a candidate, but I still had to prove to the other guys and Coach Swanson that I could be the guy who could put the team on his shoulders when the going got tough. Looking back, I think Coach Swanson was hoping I would, if not counting on me to, assume the leadership role.

At practices, I was much more confident in my junior year but still had to earn my stripes. I was six-five, a whole inch taller than the previous year, and ready for the challenges I was sure to face.

My concentration on basketball was so serious that I couldn't find time for girls—at least not enough time to get anything serious going. There were some who did not hesitate to let me know they liked me. There were some who kidded about my complexion, calling me Almond Joy. They'd say, "Your skin is like almond, and you bring me so much joy!" It was strictly in the spirit of affectionate fun and came from girls of various ethnic groups.

But I didn't know what to do with the come-ons. I was clueless. There were a couple of dates with girls I kind of liked, but I didn't have a clue as to how to pursue romance. Not only did I not have the know-how to honestly pursue girls for the purpose of going steady, I didn't have the time.

I think that is something unique to athletes. You're highly visible and opportunities abound, but the truth is that sports are so demanding, in both preparation and competition, that there is little or no time to invest in serious romantic pursuits.

No matter the sport, by the time you go through conditioning programs, practices, the season, postseason events, and commitments, at least half the year is gone. Then to make matters more complicated, at higher levels of competition, there's mandatory off-season activity to stay in shape and keep your skills sharp. Oftentimes, if there is a person an athlete likes, the average athlete will spend more time talking about them and why they think the person is so appealing rather than getting to really know them to develop a relationship. At least that's how it was for most guys back in my day.

Not only were there sports, there was school and church. I knew college was in my future, and compromising study time was not an option. I also was teaching Sunday school, and time was spent preparing for my class lessons.

Sunday school is fairly well outlined by study guides. Still, I had to make sure I read the chapters and the concordant bible verses, understood what lesson the class was supposed to get out of the chapter, and be prepared to introduce the material and lead the discussion.

The basketball team breezed through my junior year, going undefeated in the league with total domination. That year we added guard Paul Lozano, an energetic guard who was a great defender and who was really quick with the ball. His presence was a spark plug that gave us a new dynamic throughout my junior year. Our only loss prior to the postseason competition was an opening season nonleague shellacking put on us by Notre Dame High School, which was led by prep all-American Hank Babcock.

We swept through league competition like a hot knife through butter. We beat our rival Oxnard by 27 and 20 points: 97–70 in one game and 94–74 in the other. Although we were more pumped for Oxnard, we actually got tighter games from neighboring Santa Barbara High School. Santa Barbara was the big dog in football but also was a pretty enthusiastic basketball community. They played well against us, but we were able to beat them in two low-scoring games: 56–33 and 54–47.

We were ranked fourth in the California Interscholastic Federation 4A Division. We had an excellent shot at the championship. The only problem was that the road to the CIF championship went through Compton and the legendary coach Bill Armstrong, with a highly talented and athletic roster that included Renaldo Brown, Louie Nelson and Mr. Larry Hollyfield.

Compton already had won two consecutive CIF Southern Section Championships and was very experienced in championship-tournament competition where every possession is important and everything you do for four quarters has a major impact on the outcome of every possession. Plus, Compton would expose any weakness a team had.

When a team wins a championship, particularly consecutive championships, they develop a swagger. They have an abundance of confidence and concentration, and they know each man can and will play hard and smart on every possession. When you have that going for you, you can beat a physically superior team—and sometimes a more talented team. That's not to say we were more talented than Compton was, but we had enough going for us to match up fairly. Nevertheless, Compton was a close contest, 56–51, en route to capturing yet another CIF championship. To this day, Coach Swanson believes that we could have beaten them if we'd had the kind of top-level championship-tournament experience that Compton had. They simply knew how to get it done.

We had three players among the top ten in scoring in the Channel League. Robert Turner was the league's top scorer. I was second, and Glenn Hannah was sixth.

I was voted Channel League Player of the Year. I also received most-valuable-player honors in the Beverly Hills tournament earlier that season.

I had averaged 20.1 points a game while racking up numerous other honors. I also was able to maintain my status as an honor student, and I was elected president of the Ventura High School Student Body Association.

I already had been well established as a national blue-chipper, a high-school player who has the potential to be an immediate asset to any top-level college program. I had been contacted by hundreds of colleges and had narrowed my choices down to five. My final five were USC, Stanford, Harvard, Pennsylvania, and UCLA.

As a sophomore, I had an opportunity to meet some of the big UCLA stars when Danny and Duane Roberts and myself were invited to attend some of the parties their brother Virgil Roberts would throw when he attended UCLA. I got to meet Lew Alcindor (Kareem Abdul-Jabbar), Lucius Allen, and Mike Warren.

They really were some great parties. There was a lot of group rhythm and interaction, like singing with the songs, clapping, and soul-train lines. The finger-poppin' was so cool, guys would be giving each other high fives while boppin' and groovin' with their dance partners.

At one party, I had a slow dance with this absolutely gorgeous, tall, young lady. The dance was made memorable by her holding me tightly. We danced to the ballad "Stay" by legendary rhythm and blues group the Dells. We had this nice smooth rhythm going. After the dance, I was wowed, thinking, "Yeah, UCLA is pretty cool." The lady was a person I had never seen before or since, but that's the kind of thing that made those parties special.

But even partying with the nationally famous UCLA Bruins basketball stars while they were riding the crest of repetitive championships, and even with the heavenly coeds and the glitter of Tinseltown, UCLA was not my number-one choice. Had I made a decision on which college to attend after my junior year, it would have been Stanford.

However, before I had a chance to deliberate on my five college choices, I had a more immediate situation develop.

My dad had accepted an opportunity to become pastor of Second Baptist Church in Santa Barbara. My family was moving thirty miles north.

The Santa Barbara move did not present a difficult problem at the outset. As the pastor of Olivet Baptist Church in Ventura for eleven years, my family was well entrenched in the Ventura community, and there was no problem with my finding a place to stay to finish my senior year at Ventura High. In fact, just about everyone I knew, including my mother, wanted me to remain in Ventura.

In addition to family friends and a few other places available for me to stay, Coach Swanson had a housing opportunity for me with a friend of his. I also had a chance to stay with my good friend Terry Knight. So at the outset, there was never a question of whether I would stay but where.

One of my choices was a lady, Mrs. Beatrice Wyatt, a close friend of the family who had just given my dad a car that was seldom used. It was a 1950 kelly-green Oldsmobile, which my dad passed along to me. She was kind of a den-mother of the church who offered room at her home for me, and lived alone. She was employed as a domestic and not home a lot. I figured that would be the ideal situation. It provided me with the most privacy and freedom.

So the family moved on up the road to Santa Barbara, and I stayed behind.

Although the question of where I would stay was topical and made for interesting conjecture on my having a small degree of independence, when the family actually moved, I felt dramatically different. I was not at all comfortable without my family. It occurred to me that this could be my last year at home, because I would be going away for college the following year.

But my host, the Swanson family, and other family friends helped to take the edge off of the emotions I had being away from my family.

I also got a summer job at West Park in Ventura, and that helped a lot.

Everything was going well. Then, there were two street-related incidents that served as catalysts for me to reconsider things in a different light.

Both incident involved girls.

Both incidents involved guns.

One occurred during an outing I had with my buddies Al Haynes and Vernon Mitchell. Vernon was a track star.

Al was one of the charmers that girls found handsome, and he was a big star on our football team. He was definitely a lady's man for the ages and could charm the skin off a snake. Girls didn't swoon over him; they genuinely liked him as a nice guy. He was not a slick street type, just an engaging, personable fellow.

On this particular occasion, I was driving my 1950 Oldsmobile. It handled more like a truck, but to me it was as cool as a convertible sports car. Al and Vernon were hanging out with me.

Al was in the front seat; Vernon was in the back.

Al and Vernon both had eyes for this girl named Rachel.

Rachel's name came up during the conversation.

Vernon, all of sudden, said to Al, "I want you to leave her alone."

Al glanced back over his shoulder, and his eyes got real big. That startled expression caused me to look back.

What we saw was Vernon with a gun. I just about crapped! I didn't know what to think. Two things crossed my mind.

One was the hope that Vernon would not shoot.

Two, if he did, I hoped he would remember the matter was between he and Al!

Al and I were tight partners, and I would go to the end of the earth for him. But at that moment, the end of the earth was upon us. I had a flash-forward vision of the next morning's headline: "Ventura High Basketball Star Keith Wilkes Shot." I was getting sicker. I was inches and possibly seconds away from being history.

It was a good thing that Al was a quick thinker, because I was in shock and holding my breath, waiting for execution.

Before an argument ensued, Al played down his relationship with Rachel, saying she was Vernon's girl and that he (Al) was only clowning with her. I nodded my head yes in accordance with Al's lead, hoping Vernon was going to go along with what Al was saying. He bought it. Whew! That put the situation to rest, and we proceeded to have fun that evening.

The other pistol incident related to this girl who attended Oxnard High School but who frequently came to our games to see me play. I didn't know much about her, other than the fact that she was a senior and a couple of years older than I was.

She usually had her eyes glued on me and made some overtures, but I didn't know what to do with her. The guys would give me the business about her. She was very attractive, so I found it all amusing. In my mind, I had two words for their jiving about a mythical relationship between her and me: "I wish!"

One Saturday evening, I was doing some sweeping while closing the park when these two guys came in. They appeared to be under the influence of something. This one guy, Tony, had been pursuing this girl and was following her around while she was following me around. He apparently had considered her his girlfriend.

They approached me. It was a scene right out of the movie *Westside Story*: tough guys determined to make a statement.

"Hey Keith, I want you to quit messing around with my girl," Tony demanded with a commando attitude.

I didn't have a girlfriend and didn't know how to get one. I didn't have the nerve to even approach the ones I did like. And I didn't know what this guy was talking about, although, frankly, it was becoming clear. I was about to get jumped on and beat up because this guy believed I was fooling around with *his* girlfriend. His allegations started coming together in a form that I could understand, but it was all news to me. Since I had no relationship with the girl in question, I was more dumbfounded regarding the part about me being involved with her.

I was never a street fighter, and I certainly did not want to try and become one at that point with the odds against me: two thuggish-looking guys against a skinny choir boy. Yep, I was scared.

After analyzing my situation and complete disadvantage, I thought it best to try to get a handle on what was going on, so I asked the obvious question: "What girl?"

Bzzzz—wrong response!

It came across as though I was ignoring his demand.

Commando Tony then got belligerent and began to fly off at the handle. He was under the influence—I now clearly recognized—emotional, and had a lot of anxiety. He didn't know what to do, and he started to charge me.

He stopped about four feet from me and pulled out a gun.

At this point, his buddy all of sudden got excited and tried to stop him.

Since his buddy appeared surprised, it was clear things had gotten out of control. We were well beyond any words from me that could possibly help the situation. More headlines: "Basketball Star Keith Wilkes Gunned Down."

I was silent as a rock. My mind notified me that my life had been pinked slipped and that I was going to die for a girl I never got the chance to know. You could hear my heart pounding. There was no scenario in which I would have wanted a confrontation with either of these guys, even in a fair fight, and there I was with a gun pointed at me in the hand of a guy who was close enough to dance with me. My only hope was that his buddy could calm him down.

His buddy got through to him.

Tony started to get himself together. He was so wasted, I'm not sure if he realized he had pulled the gun out.

From the discussion between he and his friend, it seemed this girl had been leading him on but wasn't serious in any way. Nevertheless, he repeated his demand that I leave her alone.

I was thinking, "Now there's an idea!" I could go along with that. It was a great resolution—a pure stroke of genius—and I was perfectly willing to accommodate the notion.

"Sure. No problem," I managed to utter as though I were folding my cards at a poker game. The girl meant zero to me, so there really was no other answer to have given him. I did not feel like a chump or embarrassed in any way by conceding to this demand, but rather, I felt like I had just cut a good deal and put a big misunderstanding to rest.

The next morning I still was in shock. I promised myself to never entertain a lady who was spoken for or remotely involved in a relationship. In fact, every lady I've ever dated has had to be very clear in letting me know there wasn't a guy present in her life. I saw the girl and guy once after the incident, and that was at a basketball game at Oxnard.

With those successive near fatal occurrences, the whole notion about semi-independence seemed like a little larger step into the future than what I was ready for. It made me rethink Santa Barbara and being with my family my last year before going away to college.

I was able to shake off the gun-related incidents, but I couldn't shake off the desire to be with my family. I made a very independent decision to be with my family. It is a decision I would make today, a thousand times over. As it turned out, it was, indeed, my last year at home.

Without hardly any effort, Coach Swanson could have persuaded me to stay in Ventura. It is often said that coaches are like fathers away from home, and in some cases, they are surrogate fathers. Coach Swanson and I certainly had that kind of relationship. Plus, my parents had a tremendous amount of respect and admiration for him. And it was Mom who was encouraging me to stay in Ventura—if that was what I wanted.

But Coach Swanson clearly understood the dilemma, probably better than I did. He would never have used any arm-twisting tactics like reminding me how close

Ventura was to a CIF championship and that I would
be letting the team down. We had been knocking on the
championship door for two years. I was a senior, the
man, and on the surface of things, the championship was
just sitting there for us to take. All he had to do was say,
"Keith, I think you should stay." And that would have
been that.

I'm proud that I made the right decision, but I am
equally proud that I went to Coach Swanson first. From a
pure basketball perspective, he was the one who would be
most negatively affected, and I cared about his reaction.
It was unimaginable that I would not play at Ventura
my senior year and go out with a bang, but without my
family, I was a fish out of water.

"Coach," I said, "I really want to stay, but I also really
want to spend my last year on a daily basis with my
brother, my mom, and my dad."

Coach Swanson showed his usual uniquely compas-
sionate character, and with great sensitivity, he told me
he was disappointed but prepared.

As far as changes in my social life, living in Santa
Barbara wasn't difficult at all. We had relatives there,
and I had been visiting frequently. In fact, I had many
friends at Santa Barbara High School. One was Sam
Cunningham, who went on to become a USC Trojan
and NFL star running back. He had three brothers:
Bruce, Anthony, and Randall. Randall became a big star
quarterback with the Philadelphia Eagles and Minnesota
Vikings. Sam actually graduated the year before I arrived
in Santa Barbara.

I was to learn later that Coach Swanson didn't think Ventura had a shot at the title, even had I stayed. We would have had four new starters on the team. I don't know if he said that to ease my conscience, but I think we could have won it all.

HIGHLY RECRUITED BLUE CHIP – Prospective colleges were narrowed down to UCLA, Stanford, Harvard and Cal Berkeley (I was born in Berkeley). Coach Wooden sealed the deal with a personal visit to my home and a bonding between he and my brother Leo, which impressed my mother.

V

THE STRESS OF THE RECRUITING PROCESS

Before I set sail for my recruiting visit to Harvard, we had a visitor to our house—a college recruiter who took my mom, my brother, Leo, and I out to dinner. He was a humble person who didn't promise anything. My mother was most impressed by the fact that he actually paid more attention to my brother, Leo, and showed that he knew a lot about human nature. The man's name was John Wooden.

My transferring to Channel League rival Santa Barbara High School created a huge stir in both Ventura and Santa Barbara, as well as throughout the CIF basketball community in Southern California.

The two cities are thirty miles apart. They are both very similar communities. Each is a small, very suburban coastal city located right along US Highway 101 and just northward up the road from Los Angeles, Santa Monica, and Malibu.

I hadn't worked out much at all during the summer of 1969 while heading into my senior year. Having been on the fence about moving to Santa Barbara, having worked a little bit, and experienced some threatening situations in the streets, my head was in a twilight zone. Nevertheless, I was very sure about everything else in terms of long-range plans, and my priorities were well placed.

With the controversial buzz going strong about my transferring to Santa Barbara, I became aware of my basketball skills being something of value. I was not just a good player; I was a treasured player who was coveted. It was now show time—time for me to turn it on for the paying public.

Everyone was excited during my first day of school. Jeremy Kramer, the student-body president of Santa Barbara, offered to share his presidency with me since I had been elected student-body president at Ventura.

There was a Black Student Union, and the students invited me to get involved. Since I had already known a few people in the community, I became very comfortable right away.

However, I politely declined all extracurricular activities. I had a one-track mind: have a good basketball year, make good grades, and move on to college.

About the only adjustment that became a concern was my new coach, Jack Triguerio, the uncle of my friend Tony Triguerio in Ventura.

Coach Triguerio was well respected throughout the league, and his coaching alone kept his teams competitive. In Santa Barbara, he was as revered as Coach Swanson was in his neck of the woods. That's where the similarities ended. He was substantially, if not completely, different than Coach Swanson.

Coach Triguerio was a former drill sergeant in the US Army. He was also once a bouncer at a bar. His personality, in my opinion, was combative. The great USC football legend Sam Cunningham tried to play basketball for him the year before but left the team because he didn't have a good relationship with the coach.

He wasted little time trying to intimidate me. Overall, he seemed pleased with having me there, but he also had a reputation to uphold.

Although we did not have a close relationship, I later learned that he had been my strongest advocate in the Channel League Player of the Year voting after my sophomore year. I learned that, in a meeting of Channel League coaches, he pushed to have me selected. The actual decision was left solely to Coach Swanson since he had the league-championship team and was coach of the two top candidates. As is customary with most high-school coaches, the nod in tight decisions will go to the upperclassman, and Danny Roberts was named MVP that year.

During one of our first encounters, he came on very strong and very tough: "Have you been working out? Have you been lifting weights? Have you been running?"

His psychological intimidation didn't penetrate my own sense of purpose. I was very much aware that I was a national blue-chipper and that I already had a future beyond Santa Barbara High School. The summer had been complicated, and my workout activities were inconsistent, but I was in good shape and always ready to rock and roll on a basketball court, so I saw no need to kowtow. I told the coach that I was just getting settled into school and that I wanted to ease into things.

With the tempo of our relationship having been set, needless to say, I didn't have the same rapport with Coach Triguerio as I had, and continued to have, with Coach Swanson.

My general attitude was that I was valued property going into a new situation as a star, but that star status had nothing to do with the kind of person I was. So I chose to deal with the dilemma of this relationship in a businesslike manner. Another truism is that, just as my staying at Ventura could have led to a CIF championship, my going to Santa Barbara increased Coach Triguerio's chances of reaching the top.

My personal perspective was one of tunnel vision. My theme was: *I came to get off and get out.* To achieve that, I had to do well academically beyond anything else. I made a very conscious decision that I wasn't going to extend myself with extracurricular activities unless it was something in the interest of my future plans.

I had already known my new teammates for quite some time, through church, the Boys Club, or interscholastic competition. I knew Alton Hayes, Dave Jackson, Bobby Thompson, and Don Ford (my future Los Angeles Lakers teammate) particularly well.

With Don, another big man, on the team, I was moved to the forward position on offense. Don played center. On defense we switched.

The other starters were Mike Macy, Dennis Muroaka and Bob Verlaan. Another outstanding performer for us was Bobby Thompson, who started several games, along with Dave Jackson.

Since Verlaan was the only returning Santa Barbara letterman, there wasn't too much in the way of high expectations. However, it was widely thought that we'd do well, and there was quite a bit of interest in how I would contribute. I was already considered one of the most outstanding players ever to compete in prep basketball in the area.

SANTA BARBARA HIGH SCHOOL DONS – (L-R) Dennis Muroka, Alton Hayes, Bob Verlaan, Louie Tomberg, Ron Murell, Coach Triguero, Keith Wilkes, Don Ford, Mike Macy, Bruce Crist, Bob Demetriou, Bob Thompson, Dave Jackson.

I got out of the box with a bang.

Here's what *Santa Barbara News-Press* sportswriter
John Nadel wrote in the December 11, 1969, edition after
our first game, an 81–42 win over Cabrillo:
"Keith Wilkes, playing his first game for the Dons, didn't
disappoint those watching. The 6'6" senior, an All-CIF
performer for Ventura High last year, scored 27 points,
grabbed 14 rebounds, and handed out six assists. Wilkes
sat out more than 10 minutes of play as all of the Dons
saw extensive action."

Don Ford also had a great game, scoring seventeen
points.

And in our second win, a 71–49 victory over
Burroughs High of Burbank: "Senior Keith Wilkes has
another banner night with thirty-three points, eighteen
rebounds, and four assists."

My initial two-game totals were sixty points, thirty-
two rebounds, and ten assists.

The headline following our third game in the
December 17, 1969, edition of the *News-Press*, "Wilkes'
Big Second Half Helps Dons Defeat Royals," led off a
story about our 78–48 win over San Marcos High School.
I had twenty-six points (making it eighty-six for the first
three games), fifteen rebounds, and four assists.

That's how things went. After an 82–49 win over
Bishop Amat (where college football TV analyst, former
USC Trojan, and Los Angeles Rams star quarterback Pat
Hayden attended), the *News-Press* stated, "Santa Barbara's
Keith Wilkes stands head and shoulders above. The classy
six-six forward literally controlled both backboards and
scored twenty-six points."

As fate would have it, the first time we played against my former team, Ventura, I was sick the entire week before the game and missed a few days of school. There was quite a bit of talk about the game, and I had a lot of anxiety myself.

Ventura had dominated the Channel League for the last several years, and everyone knew that, despite my absence, they were going to be tough. Nevertheless, I was ready by game time. We won 63–48. I scored thirty-three points, but more importantly, Don Ford and I were working together extremely well.

We breezed through the league, beating everybody by twenty or thirty points. We were the number-one-ranked team in the CIF going into the play-offs.

Our first play-off game was against Santa Monica High School. The game was sold out in advance. They even added more seats. We won easily, 74–61.

Our second play-off game was against the number-three-ranked team in the CIF, Morningside High of Inglewood, and a perennial championship-caliber team. There was a quirk in the scheduling, and the number-one and number-three teams had to meet early in the play-offs.

Morningside was going to be a lot tougher challenge. We had not played a close contest since a 59–58 overtime victory against Righetti High School in the preseason. Nothing else was remotely close.

During the season, we had a very balanced attack, and a lot of guys got a lot of playing time. But this wasn't going to be the case against Morningside. The ball came to me a lot more. We won 58–56 in a nip and tuck contest. I scored our last thirteen points.

We advanced to the quarterfinal game, where we met up with prep all-American Hank Babcock and Notre Dame High, which had beaten my Ventura team badly the year before. The game was played before six-thousand-plus wild and frenzied fans as we moved deeper into the play-offs. This time, the table turned, and we won. I scored twenty-five points, with fifteen rebounds and six assists. Babcock had nineteen points, mostly free throws.

Coming back with that strong win, after a close game over Morningside, brought our confidence back up and gave us a little swagger. We could smell the roses.

At practice the Tuesday before the semifinal game, Coach Triguerio challenged me to a one-on-one match. As a basketball player, a one-on-one game is always fine, but I was detecting that he was riding high on our date with destiny and wanted to assert himself by taking on the person at the center of attention. That would be me!

We began playing innocently enough. He was playing me pretty rugged, so I kind of stayed outside.

On a missed shot, I went for the rebound. In his aggressive play, he initiated body contact as I was still in the air, and when I came down, I landed on his foot. The awkward landing caused my ankle to twist. A severely sprained ankle resulted. It kept me out of practices the rest of the week. The semifinal game was Friday.

We were slated to play Millikan High School of Long Beach. With another huge crowd of 7,215, we lost

66–53. The headline in the *News-Press* the next day read, "Dons' Title Drive Ends With 66–53 Millikan Ambush."

The writer reported, "A combination of excellent Millikan play, coupled with a flat performance by most of the Dons players on the same night when brilliant forward Keith Wilkes was not at his superlative best because of a sprained ankle..."

Coach Triguerio was quoted: "Keith went out and played as hard and as well as he possibly could under the circumstances."

The article continued, "Despite the ankle sprain, the six-six senior forward still was the best player on the court."

I had been double-teamed and harassed all night and finished with seventeen points and twelve rebounds.

There was never any doubt that, without the sprained ankle, I would have played better, there would have been a different outcome, and we would have won it all. Millikan went on to win the CIF championship.

I managed to break a couple of Santa Barbara single-season records set by Vic Bartolome, a seven-footer who went on to play for Oregon State a few years earlier, and a few years in the NBA after being drafted by the Golden State Warriors in 1970. He also played in Europe in Livorno, Italy and later with ZZ Leiden, The Netherlands, winning the 1979 Dutch National Championship.

I had 651 points, breaking the previous mark of 576. I had 427 rebounds, breaking the previous record of 289.

I was selected the CIF Southern Section Player of the Year. For the second straight year, the Channel League coaches voted me the Channel League Player of the Year.

I had averaged twenty-four points and sixteen rebounds per game.

I was selected to several all-American teams. On many of those all-American teams were my future UCLA teammates Bill Walton and Greg Lee, and future NBA stars Jan Van Bredda Koff, Tom McMillan, and Len Elmore. Elmore was from Power Memorial High School, where Kareem Abdul-Jabbar attended.

The only remaining issue was my choice of college.

Bill Walton, Greg Lee, and I visited Stanford together.

We met the basketball players and many other Stanford athletes, including football heroes Jim Plunket and Gene Washington.

I was really interested in Stanford, mainly because I had relatives in the area. I was born in Berkeley, and as noted earlier, my sister Naomi was attending school there, while my other sister Gail was at nearby University of San Francisco.

Bill, Greg, and I easily became friends and made a pact to all go to the same school.

Greg's dad had attended UCLA, which was a big influence for him, and it was emerging as Bill's top choice.

I had been in communication with Denny Crum, the assistant coach at UCLA. Like most people, I was in awe of their strong run of NCAA championships.

As a high-school kid, I was really enjoying all of the recruiting activity. The University of Pennsylvania was on my short list. I flew to Philadelphia and met with Coach Dick Harter and their big star, Corky Calhoun, who later played with the Portland Trailblazers. Dave Wohl, a future NBA coach, was also on that team.

I really liked Coach Harter a lot, but I found Philadelphia too cold. And that was just the spring weather.

Next on my agenda was a trip to Cambridge, Massachusetts, to check out Harvard University.

Dad was very enthusiastic about the possibility of my going to Harvard. Parents want the best for their kids, and for those with strong academic promise, Harvard is usually on the list or somewhere in the family conversation.

Personally, I had long been impressed with the stature of the Ivy League. David Lawyer, my high-school basketball idol, was at Princeton, and Virgil Roberts was now attending law school at Harvard. The thought of going to Harvard University was also euphoric to me, as well as Dad. All things equal, Harvard would have been the school.

But as a promising collegiate basketball player, there was still the consideration of a school with a big-time basketball program, particularly since I was being heavily recruited.

But before I set sail to visit Harvard, we had a visitor come to our house. He was a college recruiter who took my mom, my brother, Leo, and I out to dinner. He had insisted that Leo come along. Dad was busy that particular evening.

We went to an exclusive restaurant on the Santa Barbara pier. We talked about things in general.

He was a humble person who didn't promise anything. My other recruiting conversations addressed my being an impact on the program. Some even had projections of how successful I would be after a four-year stint. According to them, I was going to be a huge success and seemingly already in their institution's Hall of Fame.

This guy simply stated that he thought I could fit into his program nicely but that I would have to earn the opportunity.

Up to that point, although I was enjoying all the traveling, attention, and entertaining, I had been treated pretty much like a prize catch and a piece of property for the respective basketball programs.

This was different. Academics, study habits, and hard work were words not as prevalent in any other conversation.

My mother was most impressed by the fact that he actually paid more attention to my brother, Leo, and showed that he knew a lot about human nature.

The man's name was John Wooden.

With the exception of a courtesy trip to Harvard, to fulfill my promise to visit them, the case was closed. I was going to UCLA. Greg and Bill were already committed, and I added my name immediately so far as the Pacific-8 League (now Pac-12) was concerned. I couldn't say absolutely, positively until after my previously planned trip to Harvard.

There was a lot of interest in where I would attend college. Locally, with the tremendous popularity of UCLA basketball, there was considerable speculation and hopes that I would go there. College basketball enthusiasts supporting other colleges on my short list were hoping likewise.

Interestingly, UCLA's star forwards, Sidney Wicks and Curtis Rowe, were a year away from graduation, making a perfect roadway for me to possibly move into the rotation or a starting forward spot in my sophomore year. At that time, freshmen were not eligible to play college-varsity basketball.

With such widespread community interest and the decision-making process heating up, the *Santa Barbara News-Press* kept pace on a daily basis. An article appeared in the April 4, 1970, edition, stating, "Wilkes plans to attend either UCLA or Harvard...he signed a Pac-8 letter of intent but was flying back to Harvard. Wilkes has an A-minus grade point average and is one of the most heavily recruited players in the state. He was named to three all-American teams."

I had promised the sports reporter that I would make my decision after my Harvard trip, and I made the announcement on Cinco de Mayo (May 5). On May 6, the *News-Press* headline gave the locals the good news: "It's Official. Wilkes Definitely Going to UCLA."

I was quoted in the article: "'Everything I'm interested in is offered at UCLA,' Wilkes said. 'This includes academic opportunities, prospects after graduation, and basketball.'"

The recruitment and decision-making process proved draining—more so than I had been aware. Afterward, I felt as though I was suffering from delirium. Upon returning from Harvard, I scheduled a visit with the family physician, Dr. Paul Fillmore. My parents thought I might have been a little ill, but I just went to talk with him. I kind of babbled, and that was the moment of my final decision to go to UCLA.

I don't recall the game, but I later learned Coach wooden had come to one of my games with Coach Crum, who was recruiting me. I didn't have one of my better games and Coach wooden was not impressed at all. In fact, I was told, he was displeased with having given up an evening with his family to make the two-hour trip up the coast. Coach Crum was persistent and able to convince him to come to a second game and it was a much better game for me the second time around.

I went home, sat quietly in my room, and then called my parents in to discuss my proposed final decision. With their consent, it was off to the University of California at Los Angeles.

UCLA freshman (Jamaal) Keith Wilkes

VI

APPROACHING ACADEMIC CHALLENGES AT UCLA

My two biggest problems at the outset were finding a parking place and finding my way to class. Another adjustment was that UCLA was on a quarter system, which is a ten-week period that seems to zoom by. The most interesting and stimulating adjustment was getting comfortable with being around people who were very academically competitive and very motivated.

With the decision to go to UCLA, there was a tremendous release of pressure.

It was difficult turning away from Stanford, because I had often thought I would probably land in the Bay Area. I thoroughly enjoy the Bay Area, and just as much as wanting to make my parents proud, I also wanted to make my sisters proud. I was directly influenced by their academic achievements, and it seemed that following their footsteps in higher-education years would ensure my continued success. Plus, they would have been a great support for me in meeting athletic expectations.

With Harvard and Pennsylvania, I was infatuated by the prestige and academic aura of the Ivy League. Just the idea that I was Ivy League quality and had an open option to go to a couple of Ivy League schools was exhilarating. Most students who work hard to excel academically have at least a notion, if not a desire, to be Ivy League quality. They may opt for Duke, Vanderbilt, Stanford, Georgetown, or Northwestern, but chances are that there is an Ivy League school they wouldn't mind attending.

But UCLA would provide all of the above. My parents, family and friends, and other folks who I spent the previous six years around would only be a short drive away, and that meant a lot. UCLA was far enough away from home but yet close enough to get home on holidays or extended weekends. Plus, my parents and brother could see me play without incurring substantial expenses or airfare.

UCLA may not be an Ivy League school, or even called "the Ivy League of the West," as Stanford is affectionately known, but it has just as much academic prestige. And of course, the basketball program was the crème de la crème.

Frankly, I did not have big-time basketball aspirations, nor was professional basketball a goal. So it was easier to prioritize academics during my deliberations.

Putting it all into perspective, it actually should've been an easier process.

Going into my senior year of high school at Santa Barbara, there were some thoughts that things might not come out as envisioned, so you make sure there are options. There were risk factors in leaving Ventura High School, where I was very comfortable. The only sure thing was excelling academically. I could have been reduced to a role player on the basketball team, or I could have had a bad injury during the season, but nothing could diminish my value as college-bound student if I had the grades.

But, as it turned out, all's well that ends well. In fact, it was great. I had a great basketball year. I was slated to graduate with honors. I was going to UCLA, the premiere collegiate basketball program in the country, on a basketball scholarship. All I had to do now was enjoy the ride, continue to prioritize academics, and look forward to the future.

During the recruiting, I was just barely sixteen years old and still very naïve. It would have been easier had I not had all those options.

Options are wonderful, and better it's to have than not, but with options, there's much more second-guessing.

At first, all the recruiting and attention were flattering. There was a rush of excitement. There was a buzz in the air everywhere I went. To a small degree, there was media hype. It's hard to not get carried away, even if you are mature and levelheaded. At age sixteen, you don't stand a chance of not getting caught up unless you've committed before the season, but that reduces your options, unless you are positive about where you want to go to college, no ifs, ands, or buts.

When you realize that you have to make a major four-year decision and there's no looking back, the issue starts to intensify.

Then comes the irony that your parents try to help you by leaving you alone to make the decision!

My parents kept saying, "You're the one who'll have to live with it." (*it*, meaning the decision).

Thanks to the way they raised me and the influence of my sisters, I was self-determined. I had always been self-determined without really thinking about it. But when you hear the words that you are, in fact, on your own, self-help takes on a new perspective. The intensity increased.

Plus, I know my dad favored Harvard, and my mother was leaning toward the University of Southern California, where my sister Naomi would soon be attending law school.

It never ceases to amaze me that, when we give complicated issues an appropriate amount of thought, we often come up with the most appropriate conclusion. And there could not have been anything more appropriate than going to UCLA, one of the nation's top institutions of higher learning and whose basketball team was coming off its sixth consecutive NCAA championship.

My first concern after high-school graduation was getting a summer job.

I landed a job at Santa Barbara Cottage Hospital doing light maintenance work that included landscaping, moving and fixing beds, and some heavy-duty work, like changing light bulbs. It was a great job with great people. I'd probably be a supervisor by now had I remained. I earned enough to make my first automobile purchase, a 1964 Volkswagen Kharmen Ghia.

I didn't play much basketball that summer. The only organized event I participated in was the California North-South All-Star Game up at the University of San Francisco. The North team featured Glenn Burke, who later played with the Los Angeles Dodgers, and Phil Smith, the future standout at the University of San Francisco and a Golden State Warriors teammate of mine.

Since freshmen were not eligible for varsity basketball when I entered UCLA, I knew that the first year was to be one of adjustments. I anticipated a lot of adjustments, and it turned out to be that and more.

Although I grew up near Los Angeles, I was not familiar with city lifestyles. There were thousands of kids with very fancy cars, including Corvettes and Mercedes-Benzes.

My two biggest problems at the outset were finding a parking place and finding my way to class. Another adjustment was that UCLA was on a quarter system, which is a ten-week period that seems to zoom by.

The most interesting and stimulating adjustment was getting comfortable with being around people who were very academically competitive and very motivated. Since I didn't have varsity basketball to worry about, I dedicated myself to getting off to a good start academically and adjusting to the pace of my fellow students.

In Ventura and Santa Barbara, where most of the people knew one another, it was much more personal.

If you missed a class, your parents were apt to get a personal call at home.

UCLA, with thirty thousand–plus students, was much more impersonal.

This was a prestigious university with many nationally acclaimed professors and very competitive classes. The class sizes were extremely large in comparison to high school. You had to get yourself there on time, and you had to get the information.

With such large classes, a quarter system time frame, and being at an academically challenging university, there was not time for professors to be personal. In high school, teachers are dedicated to helping you reach the next level. At a university, the information for you to get to the next level of life is there, but you got to get it. If you'd rather waste your tuition money and opportunity to become well positioned in life, that's fine too. Even the graduate teaching assistants didn't have much time to be personal. However it was that you wanted to succeed in class, you had to go get it.

Obviously, the only way to get any attention was by being aggressive and keeping up with the competition. The competition didn't come from kids who lived around the corner from your home or in the next subdivision or who went to church with you. It came from people from different cities, countries, and cultures. You may have to compete with a math genius from Japan, an Ethiopian who studies every waking hour, an Australian with an IQ of 145, or a Jewish kid from Missouri who scored 1600 on her SAT. You can never really get ready for that kind of academic environment;

you just have to be prepared to adjust to it once you get there.

Freshman eligibility was then a major topic, but not being eligible for varsity basketball as a freshman was a major asset to me, personally speaking. It set the table for my four years at UCLA. Of course the culture has advanced to where, today, we have one-and-done freshmen who go into college NBA-ready.

As a regular student, I was able to learn the system and make the transition to college. I had a great foundation in Ventura and dedicated myself during my senior year at Santa Barbara. That obviously enabled me to make the appropriate adjustments. Once I knew the game plan and the level of competition, I was all right, and the result was that, when I graduated from UCLA, I had a 3.6 grade point average and a bachelor of science degree in economics. I must give credit to the UCLA athletic department that made tutorial support services available and Coach Wooden's mantra on getting an education. Coach Wooden was dogmatic about prioritizing academic affairs.

The education I received prepared me well for the business world.

Circumstances vary widely on an individual basis, but for the majority of student athletes, I think freshman eligibility increases the degree of difficulty for making an adjustment to college academia. There are some student athletes who are bright enough to fit right in, and there certainly are some whose talent level warrants them to play right away. However, the number of people it hinders outweighs the number of people it helps.

There are a lot of demands on major college coaches to win. The late Al Davis, who was owner and president of the Oakland Raiders, said it best: "Just win, baby. Win." The same level of competitiveness exists at the college level, and, in fact, there are college coaches whose jobs and career depend on winning seasons.

With that kind of pressure, freshmen eligibility becomes larger than life. Add to that the pressure of the economic rewards for the university if it gets into NCAA tournaments or for the players if they get postseason honors. It is hard to prioritize academics with those kinds of pressures. Freshmen should be given an opportunity to make all the necessary adjustments and begin formulating their life goals.

Admittedly, when I started at UCLA, the economic stakes were not so grand. Hardship opportunities for the more talented players to shorten their collegiate careers and go pro were just beginning. The only hardship case to speak of was Spencer Haywood. Spencer is to basketball what Curt Flood is to baseball. Though Haywood's issue dealt with player drafts opening the door for underclassmen and Flood's dealt with players' rights relative to trades and opened the door for free agency and trade-refusal rights, both changed the landscape of how professional-sports organizations acquire athletes.

In 1969, Spencer left the University of Detroit after his sophomore year and challenged the NBA rules blocking the drafting of underclassmen and high-school players. He eventually signed with Denver in the American Basketball Association and played fourteen seasons in both the ABA and NBA. The next guy was Moses Malone, who actually had enrolled in the University of Maryland in 1974. A three-million-dollar contract offer from the Utah Stars of the ABA helped him change his mind about playing for the Terrapins at Maryland.

Later, Earvin "Magic" Johnson would come out after his sophomore year at Michigan State, and he would show just how thrilling and impacting a young marketable player can be in the NBA. Earvin opened the marketing floodgates for corporate America that set the stage for others, like Michael Jordan and Kobe Bryant to take product endorsements to astronomical heights. Jordan, of course, came out of North Carolina after his junior year, and Bryant passed by college ball all together.

Today, of course, in basketball, there're more and more players who will go directly into the draft, and several who will come out after their first or second year of college. You'd like to see people excel academically, but it's a new day, and if they can get a million bucks within days after accepting their high-school diploma, it's a no-brainer.

But during the years I was in college, hardship was not an option often thought of by college athletes. So everyone during this time period was thinking of graduation. At least I was.

Coach John Wooden

VII

THE BRUIN WAY

He never gave way to being abusive in any form. But if you were just going through the motions, that could get his attention. In that case, he would give you a kind reminder: invite you to sit down and replace you on the floor with another all-American. His actions spoke louder than words.

The overwhelming media hyperbole concerning NCAA basketball and the NCAA Championship Tournament was nothing like it is today, but UCLA basketball commanded a lot of national attention.

There was good reason: John Wooden. As the saying goes, "Good water trickles from the top," and Coach Wooden's personal success and coaching excellence had a trickle-down effect on his teams and players. Coach had been a successful player and coach, *and* while serving as a lieutenant in the US Navy, he was a flight instructor,

so he had a distinctive feel for teaching and motivating
men.

You'd never know it, because he doesn't pound his
chest about it, but Coach Wooden has a humanity orien-
tation that truly reflects his belief in equality and human
rights. As a coach in his earlier years at Indiana State, he
had a team that went 29–7 and was set to challenge for the
National Association of Intercollegiate Athletics (NAIA)
Championship. But the NAIA would not allow Indiana
State to compete for the championship in Kansas City
because they had a black player. Coach Wooden refused
to play.

His success at Indiana State and previous success at
South Bend Central High School (218–42) caught the
attention of major colleges, and he was much sought
after. The chief suitors were the University of Minnesota
and UCLA.

Folklore has it that John Wooden was not UCLA's
first choice, but in reality, UCLA wasn't John Wooden's
first choice.

He had chosen Minnesota because he wanted to remain
in the Midwest. However, as they were about to finalize
the contract via telephone at a designated time, a storm
knocked down the power lines, the call was delayed, and
the contract consummation never took place. Meanwhile,
he went ahead and accepted the UCLA job.

After going 22–7 in his first year at UCLA, he was
offered a job during his second year to return home and
coach his alma mater, Purdue University. But he had
signed a three-year contract, and his belief in loyalty and

honesty kept him from entertaining the notion of leaving UCLA.

In 1939, he first created the famous Pyramid of Success philosophy, his character-development blueprint for those who had the desire and will to be successful on and off the court, and refined it over the years.

As a basketball coach, he designed it so that his players easily could relate to the building-block principles for teamwork and achievement, as well as codes of conduct. In fact, he is a pioneer among those in sports who place an equal emphasis on conduct away from the basketball court or playing field as they do on it.

His emphasis on character came from a lesson he learned as a youngster when he was the star player on his grade-school team but was benched because of a behavior issue. His team lost that day. He learned what had stuck with him throughout life: winning is not the most important thing in life.

He was my coach and mentor, but he was also an idol because he had accomplished everything that I was trying to achieve.

I aspired to be a scholar athlete. He was a heralded scholar athlete at Purdue University.

I aspired to be a major contributor to an NCAA championship team. Coach Wooden had been there and done that. In 1932, he was the College Player of the Year. I wanted to live an exemplary life in the model that my father had set for me, and Coach Wooden was all that. In 1964, he was the California Father of the Year. In 1970, he was the *Sporting News* Sportsman of the Year, and in 1971, he was named the Friar's Club Coach of the Century.

He won his first national championship in 1964 with a team that did not have a player over six-five. As my class stepped into the varsity limelight, Coach Wooden was riding six consecutive NCAA championships. And the Wicks-Patterson-Rowe team left us with a win streak of fifteen games.

What was equally remarkable was that the coach himself was such an outstanding leadership player. He had led Martinsville (Indiana) High School to a state championship. Long before Larry Bird became a legend in Indiana, there was John Wooden. He was a three-time all-American guard and captain of the Purdue team that won the Big Ten titles in 1931 and 1932 and the 1932 NCAA championship. Ironically, he did not attend Purdue on scholarship. He was there during the Great Depression years and had to work and pay his own way through.

His name was inscribed on Purdue's academic honor roll, and he was awarded the 1932 Big Ten Conference medal for outstanding merit and proficiency in scholarship and athletics.

After playing semipro and pro basketball and coaching in the high-school ranks at Dayton High (Kentucky) and South Bend Central and then his first college-level job at Indiana State, he went to UCLA in 1948.

His signature always has been up-tempo and fast-breaking teams. Coach always stressed being in great condition to be stronger and quicker at the end of the game, being fundamentally sound, and playing together as a team.

Our practices were not long, about two hours. They were concise, with drills that stressed movement, conditioning, and fundamentals. The coaching staff was very diligent in carrying out practice plans. You could see that, as a head coach, Coach Wooden believed strongly in preparation. In fact, the reason he was usually calm during the games was because he had done his best work planning practices and his best coaching at practices.

I always saw him as a patient man. He was not easy to disappoint, because he preferred aggressive play. But if you went off in your own direction, he would check that with lightening quickness.

He never gave way to being abusive in any form. But if you were just going through the motions, that could get his attention. In that case, he would give you a kind reminder: invite you to sit down and replace you on the floor with another all-American. His actions spoke louder than words.

During the summer of 1971, between my freshman and sophomore years, I worked in Santa Barbara as a construction laborer helping to build the San Marcos Pass (Highway 154).

There weren't any summer basketball programs, such as the Joe Weakley Run, Shoot, and Dunk League that came along later to give athletes a chance to work on their game in competitions. So the priority was working and earning some spare change.

The only recreation was going to visit Vince in Pasadena.

When school started back up, I rented a little room at the Fiji House on Gayley Avenue in Westwood. The Fiji House was a rooming house that enabled me to be right at the doorstep of the campus but not living in the dorms. It gave me a lot more privacy and a little more freedom.

Another student living there was Neville Garrett, who later became art director for Bob Marley and the Wailers reggae group. He was a West Indian from Kingston, Jamaica. Neville was an artist and was involved with *Nomo*, the UCLA Black Student Union publication. *Nomo* was widely read among socially conscious activists, academicians that included most African American and minority students throughout Southern California, from UC Irvine, and Cal State Fullerton, up to Cal State Northridge, and UC Santa Barbara.

Neville and I often would get together around mealtime. One of the great things about college life is that you begin to establish a new sense of family, particularly with those individuals with whom you break bread most often. Neville and I had many interesting discussions about current affairs, from Pan African and global perspectives. This was long before the Internet and global communications, so you truly had to have an academic appreciation for political, economic, geographical, theological, and cultural histories of many cultural groups, particularly for those then considered third-world countries.

Our discussions were idealistic, cosmic at times, and sometimes rhetorical because the vision we had of the world was contrary to the realities, such as racism and political differences that keep our society from being the best it can be. Most importantly, our conversations reflected our growth as students and men, our concern about our society and our environment, our understanding of economics, our ability to analyze and visualize a brighter tomorrow, and that we cared about people. It also reflected the times and was not unique to UCLA. Students across the University of California and Cal State University systems were thinking likewise, mainly at campuses in the metropolitan Los Angeles region and the Bay Area.

Prior to the start of basketball season, Coach Wooden called Bill Walton and me into his office. UCLA had won its sixth consecutive NCAA championship and was riding a fifteen-game winning streak.

Coach Wooden told us that *Sports Illustrated* wanted to do a feature story on UCLA, with focus on the two of us. It was obvious why they wanted Bill, but I was a little fuzzy as to why I was there. We had returning players who were key contributors on the 1971 championship run—like Hollyfield, Bibby, and Farmer—and there were several promising players in my class, like Vince and Greg. I had led the freshman team in scoring the year before, but in moving up to the varsity, there was a lot of competition.

Although I felt positive about things, there was no hard-core indication I was going to be an impact player. Being positive is one thing, but being overly optimistic is another. The skill level of the guys at UCLA could make you humble very quickly. So you thought more of doing the right things to contribute, rather than being a standout. Besides, practice hadn't even started.

During the discussion with Coach Wooden, I got my first real feel for him. I had known he was down to earth from his visit to Santa Barbara with my family. Now he was in total control and still very much down to earth. He was very proper! He was definitely a no-nonsense person, and he had a very simplistic approach to living and problem solving.

There were lots of pictures reflecting his achievements in his office. There was a Father of the Year plaque, photographs with presidents, photos from championship games, and so on.

The session also represented my first true coming together with Bill on a basketball court.

During our freshman year, he and Greg had basically hung out together, while Vince and I were close buddies. Gary Franklin and Hank Babcock kind of stuck together as buddies.

Entering that freshman year, Greg was the more publicized player. He was a Los Angeles City Player of the Year who was very intelligent and likeable, which made him an easy media magnate. Greg was the son of the coach of Reseda High School in Los Angeles's San Fernando Valley area, and he was a 4.0 student. He had played in the heart of metro Los Angeles regularly against the best talent, which was far better than Bill or I regularly faced.

Bill was a heralded player from the San Diego area, and I, of course, was more popular a little ways north in Ventura and Santa Barbara. So while Bill and I were

Southern Californians, we were from outside of the metro Los Angeles confines.

In addition to leading the team in scoring, I was becoming known as "Silk," a name that Greg, Bill, and Vince used frequently. The moniker actually came from a guy named Oliver, a pretty good intramural basketball player and band member who stopped by often to watch us practice.

Oliver stopped me after practice while we were dining at Dykstra Hall, where I lived as a freshman, and said, "Hey Keith, you sure look *smooth as silk* out there!"

My teammates picked up on it and plugged it in right away. It really didn't register on me, because sports nicknames rarely last more than a week. But it was better than being known as Spider, like when I was a kid.

The following year, Dick Enberg, who was then the play-by-play announcer for UCLA and the Los Angeles Rams, picked up on the Smooth-as-Silk moniker. Since then, it has stuck like glue.

Despite my freshman-year success and impetus going into sophomore year, there still were a number of excellent forwards with whom I had to compete for playing time. Hollyfield and Farmer were only juniors. Gary and Vince were sophomores, like me. Conventional wisdom said Hollyfield would be the man. He was truly a dominating force and a winner everywhere he had been, and in the later part of the 1971 season, he was showing the skills that made him a local icon in the Compton area. At any other school, he would have been competing for college player-of-the-year honors. At UCLA, he would have to settle for being a part of the puzzle to help the Bruins win championships.

So without having even one day of varsity-level practice and any kind of feel for how things were going to shake out, there I was, sitting in Coach Wooden's office and entertaining a major media-interview request.

Bill was the first to respond to the question. He simply told Coach Wooden that we hadn't done anything yet.

Coach then looked at me and asked, "What do you think, Keith?"

Bill's lead-in was great, and I couldn't have said anything wiser. I said, "I think the same way Bill does. If they want to do a story after the season, then that's great, but we haven't done anything to earn that kind of attention."

Coach seemed pleased with our decision.

Immediately after that meeting, I started to develop a clearer perspective of the phenomenon of the Bruin tradition, the legacy of John Wooden, the seven titles (five straight), and the fifteen-game winning streak.

At the first day of practice, I had a very unique feeling: I was now part of a tradition that had brought seven national titles to UCLA, but I didn't have anything to do with it.

At that first day of practice, you could hear a pin drop. Here we are, collectively as the UCLA Bruins. Everyone wanted to do well. Each of us wanted to show offensive explosiveness and defensive prowess, but most importantly, we each wanted to show that we were team players.

Among Coach's first remarks, he said, "Some of you I'm not going to like as well as others. But when you're out on the court, I'm going to look at you as a basketball player. Off the court, I will look at you as a person."

Coach Cunningham moved up as varsity assistant coach, replacing Denny Crum, who had departed to the University of Louisville.

Frankly, we had been looking forward to working with Coach Crum, who had done much of the legwork in recruiting us. But our primary concern was making a successful transition from the freshman team to the varsity squad.

Since Coach Cunningham was moving up to varsity with us, we weren't greatly impacted by Coach Crum's departure, though we did miss him. I'm not certain society, the NCAA, and member institutions included truly understand how influential a recruiting coach is on a player. How much a player likes that person has a tremendous impact on the athlete's decision, even though the player *should* make his or her choice solely on the attributes of the institution relative to their academic and other individual goals. When that recruiter moves on, as we hope he or she would do, there is a feeling that you just lost a close personal friend.

The first month of practice was very intense. The guys were bringing it.

I saw more quickness, more leaping, more ball movement, and more savvy at UCLA practices than anywhere else in my basketball life, before or after.

Once during the first week of practice my sophomore season, Coach Wooden called me over to speak with me.

I was simply terrified. The last thing you wanted was to be called over after practice, because it could not be good. "Come here, Keith," he said. "I want you to shoot shots around the key, and I'll rebound for you."

I was flabbergasted! Coach Wooden would be my personal rebounder.

Well, I must have taken about forty shots, and I was drilling it, and I remember every pass he made was perfect. Then he asked me, "Now, how does the ball leave your fingertips?"

A bit confused, I went through my windup motion again and slowed it down when it left my fingertips. Then he asked me, "Does it leave your fingertips with good reverse spin?" and demonstrated what he meant. I went through the motion again, thinking the process through, and said, "Yes." He said, "OK, you're dismissed."

Many people in media and fans have asked me how and when did I develop my unorthodox jump shot. Most young children start out on an eight-foot hoop, shooting a *sidewinder* shot just to get the ball up to the rim, and then graduate to a nine-foot hoop. When they finally get to a ten-foot hoop, they really begin to think and focus on their shooting technique. Typically, they're about thirteen or fourteen when they're strong enough to shoot consistently on a ten-foot basket.

In my case, I was six feet tall when I was eleven or twelve years old, fast, and as my skill level developed, I clearly was one of the best players of my age group. So I began to play pickup ball with guys nineteen and twenty years old who always played on ten-foot baskets and who would block my shot all the time. The last thing they wanted was to be shown up by some eleven-year-old.

I developed a technique of holding the ball behind my head and releasing it at the very last second to prevent my shot from being blocked. I didn't realize I was shooting the ball any different from anyone else. I had an inkling in high school that I may have shot differently, but my encounter with Coach Wooden underscored an interesting point. Namely, as long as the beginning and finish of your shot are orthodox and textbook and the ball goes in the basket consistently, it doesn't really much matter what happens in between.

Coach Wooden had a lot to say the first couple of weeks. But as time wore on, Coach Cunningham became more of a principal in running the practices. Although the coach was saying less, he was always right there. He always had a handful of three-by-five-inch note cards while he was overseeing the sessions. Our practices were meticulously orchestrated.

Four starters from the previous year were now gone: Steve Patterson, Sidney Wicks, Curtis Rowe, and Kenny Booker. Henry Bibby would be the only returning starter, so there were a lot of unanswered questions. Those questions were being addressed by what we demonstrated on the court in practice.

Our freshman year was great, but then again, we did not play against a team with a center the quality of ours.

Little did we know that a center the quality of Bill Walton simply did not exist.

UCLA needed a whole new front line. There was a lot of anxiety. Who's starting? Who's playing? Where do I fit in? Those were the questions running through the minds of all the players, including myself. Among the forwards, you could have reached into a hat, picked out any two guys, and had one heck of a tandem. So we were all aware that the guy next to us each day and the guy going against us each day were capable of giving UCLA a quality game as a starter. If you are not a starter, then the next question was, which forward comes off the bench first? If you weren't among the top three, you could get buried on the bench.

It wasn't long before the picture began to come into focus as to who would comprise what was known early on as Bibby's Bunch.

Bill obviously was going to start at center. Larry Farmer and I were slated to start at the forward spots. The competition at the guard position opposite of Henry was hot and heavy. It was between Greg, Tommy Curtis, and Andy Hill. Andy was a veteran from the championship team. Greg was given the nod.

Others on the roster were John Chapman, Swen Nater, Marvin Vitatoe, Gary Franklin, Larry Hollyfield, and Vince Carson. Early in the season, Carson and Curtis were our first guys off the bench. As the season wore on, Hollyfield firmly became established as the all-important sixth man.

Swen widely was considered the second best center in college basketball during our years at UCLA. He played behind Bill Walton, so he never started a game, but he went on to play professionally for fifteen years in the ABA (American Basketball Association) and NBA and had seasons in both leagues in which he led the league in rebounding.

We were well aware of the pressure on us, but we didn't do a lot of talking, other than among ourselves.

Before the games, our intensity level was sky-high. I usually became very solemn, while on the other end of the spectrum, Bill would be really pumped up.

Our external approach to things was a testimonial to Coach Wooden's recruiting. He not only went after good ball players but players with good character.

Our chemistry began to jell. We had learned the 2-2-1 full-court zone press and worked hard at it.

We wanted to perfect the 2-2-1 like no other John Wooden team had done before—or would after. Our team quickness and intensity made the 2-2-1 zone press as devastating and explosive as any offensive scheme. The science of the 2-2-1 was to gradually wear down the opposing team, physically and mentally, to make mistakes late in the game, which could lead to steals and turnovers. Sometimes this would happen immediately because of our intensity and desire to work the press to perfection.

Our principal objective was simply to apply pressure. Why let the opposing team have half the court before you apply defense? In attacking full court, we hoped to interrupt our opponent's offense immediately. Often we would get a ten-second call or turnover before they could get the ball to midcourt.

With the 2-2-1 zone press, we had people covering certain zones on the court. We would allow an easy inbound pass, and our number-one man in the zone (a guard) would take away the middle of the court and apply just enough defensive pressure to influence the ball handler to bring the ball up along the sideline. Our number-two man (the other guard) would slide over to protect the middle of the backcourt to defend the passing lane should the ball handler attempt a lateral pass.

Our three and four guys (Farmer and myself) were stationed at about the midcourt stripe at the sidelines. Our number-five man (Walton) would be back protecting the basket.

Since most ball handlers were right-handed, the ball handler would usually take the right sideline route. If he were left-handed, he would be influenced toward the left sideline route. The key to controlling the play was that he was on one sideline or the other.

As the ball handler moved down the court, the forward would step up into his pathway before he got to midcourt. With the guard to his left, the sideline to his right, and a forward (typically a taller person) in front of him, this would initiate a trap. He couldn't make the easy lateral pass because the other guard was right there in the middle of the court. The opposite forward would shift over toward the center of the court to take away an inside passing lane. At this point, the center and opposite forward became flexible, depending on where opposing players were setting themselves up on the floor. If an opposing player were setting himself deep in the far corner, the forward would stay with him, while the center would come up and take away the passing lane.

Once the trap was set, the ball handler usually panicked and would either throw a difficult pass that he would have to heave higher in the air, making it a free ball and one very easy to pick off, or he might throw an all-together errant pass that would go out of bounds or into the hands of a UCLA player smartly stationed in one of the passing lanes.

Since they only had ten seconds to get the ball over the midcourt stripe, we would give up the backward pass, because it only made it more difficult for them to beat the clock.

A ten-second call is very embarrassing. To avoid it, the ball handler, with his competitive nature, would usually attempt something, often throwing the ball away. We were able to get many turnovers and ten-second calls. The turnovers were often converted into uncontested layups or bank shots. Those plays became trademarks of Bruin blowouts. If you couldn't handle the press, the game was over before many of the fans were seated.

When a team was able to break our press and create a two-on-one break with our guys all over the court in the full-court zone, they often would be in too much of a hurry to capitalize on the situation by rushing. That was another mistake, because they often were momentarily unaware that the fifth guy back there protecting the basket was Bill Walton, who was extremely quick, agile, intense, and great at swatting shot attempts.

When there was a two-on-one break, and the one was Bill Walton, *the advantage was Bill's.* So our opponent's two-on-one break actually gave a false appearance of being an advantage.

We were well schooled in the art of reaching for the ball with palms up. Thus, we could apply maddening pressure and yet always be under control. We rarely committed reaching-in fouls while trapping. This spoke volumes for the poetry of how well we were coached, because the natural tendency on defense is to reach and claw after the ball. But Coach Wooden taught us how to stay in balance and not overreach.

Today, offenses have learned to attack the 2-2-1. Over the years, teams developed schemes to *defend* the 2-2-1 defense.

It was uniquely a UCLA strategy during the Wooden era, which always had the right blend of athletes recruited, to a large degree, to operate the 2-2-1 to perfection. Opposing teams simply could not match our team finesse and quickness because they weren't structurally built to do so.

We also were well drilled on the transition game. As a result of the repetitious practices, we never had to think when the split second came for transition. Within that same second, we were in motion going the other way, usually to score.

With our full-court 2-2-1 zone press, it would be a long time before we had a chance to find out how good of a close-game strategist Coach Wooden was because we quickly blew out the opponents. That was the ultimate strategy.

Coach Wooden used only a few different offensive sets. Since UCLA successfully recruited great athletic talent with size and quickness, the only challenge for the UCLA Bruins basketball program was fitting the parts into the system.

With the Wicks-Rowe team, Coach Wooden mostly used a double low post. Both Wicks and Rowe were great post-up players. However, on occasion, Sidney would position out on the wing, which created an option for him to take his man inside and post him up, take him off the dribble, or face up and hit the jumper. He was a dominant player at any of those options.

With our team, we alternated a low-post and high-post set. Primarily, we went with the low post because Bill was so dominant. Bill not only had no equal but hardly any threat to his rebounding and scoring abilities. He was dominant, precise, and polished.

I was often at the high post or sometimes out on the wing. Although I was far from the dominant post-up player that Sidney was, I was given the assignment of making things happen from the triple-threat position like Sidney had. We also tried to keep a low-post box for the lob pass to Larry Farmer. If he didn't score off the pass, he was very capable of posting and scoring.

The lob pass was beautiful. Ten-year-olds are doing it now, but Larry Farmer had a patent on it. All the forwards knew how to run and execute the play, and there were teams that had their own version, but no one had the signature of Larry Farmer. There was no dunking then due in large to Kareem Abdul-Jabbar's (Lew Alcindor) dominance inside, due to the no-dunking rule precipitated by Kareem Abdul-Jabbar's dominance inside. Some point to the Texas Western University's athleticism in their 1966 NCAA championship run that led to the no-dunking rule, and the arrival of Kareem at UCLA and Elvin Hayes at the University of Houston sealed the deal.

The lob pass and lay-in was the next best thing to the dunk and Larry's execution was pure art. He who would get a step on his man, circle around the box, take a high lob, and, while in the air, gracefully drop it in the bucket. Sometimes he would begin the play with the help of a screen or after faking a screen. It was the predecessor to the Coop-a-loop slam-dunk play that Michael Cooper made famous in the NBA with the Los Angeles Lakers and alley-oop that's used in many offenses from high school and AAU to colleges and pro teams.

In his lecturing during group sessions, Coach Wooden would, from time to time, talk about the principles of his Pyramid of Success philosophy. It was a sociology-based schematic encouraging us to be the best that we could be by employing the good character elements of the Pyramid of Success.

Coach also was famous for saying things like: "Be quick, but don't hurry." Meaning he wanted us to use our speed and quickness but always be under control.

"I don't want activity without achievement." Meaning we had to harness our athleticism so that we could execute efficiently as a team. Too much dribbling would be an example of activity without achievement.

"The guy who puts the ball through the hoop has ten hands." Meaning what we did on the court was a team effort. When a UCLA player scored, there was often a quick acknowledgement to the player or players who set it up. There was as much pride in making an assist or being a part of a perfect execution as there was in scoring a bucket.

Other quotes: "Failing to prepare is preparing to fail." "Things turn out for the best for those who make the best of the way things turn out." "Do not let what you cannot do interfere with what you can do." "Discipline yourself so others won't need to." "You can't let praise or criticism get to you. It's a weakness to get caught up in either one." "It's what you learn after you know it all that counts."

There were many other quotes, but my personal favorite is: "Make each day your masterpiece."

But make no mistake about it, this was all John Wooden. These were the things he taught and we practiced, the essence of his legacy—these were the things he brought to the highest level of proficiency. We were eager, willing, and ready, but it was all John Wooden.

In many of his interviews after his coaching years, he was often asked whether he thought anyone would ever have the kind of NCAA championship run he had at UCLA and whether he could do it again. He most often cited the sixty-four-team tournament field and balance of talent and said he didn't think it could be repeated. But with the way he recruited, the way he practiced, and the way he strategized, none would come close to repeating what he accomplished. There are programs like North Carolina, Kansas, Kentucky, UConn, Duke, and Indiana, to name a few, that have recruited well and established lasting legacies of winning programs, but winning eight straight NCAA championships through a grueling sixty-four-team balanced tournament field is another thing.

Coach Wooden did not run a democracy. It was a definite monarch, and in reverence and affection, we easily could see he was king. He was wise beyond his place in time, and he knew his players and their abilities better than we knew ourselves. He was more than a college basketball coach. He was a highly skilled technician in the art of teaching the game, maintaining the highest level of competitive readiness, and strategically coaching all facets of the game.

UCLA teams under Coach Wooden most often had superior talent that executed with exact precision, like poetry in motion. He didn't believe in altering our game plan for any one team. From day one to the end of the season, we worked on what we did as a team, without regard to whom we would be playing. We worked a lot on defense. It was his philosophy that defense is more constant, while offense can be hot or cold.

I certainly found that to be very true.

Whenever I found myself having an off night at the college or professional level, I would work harder on defense or rebounding. By doing so, I could create scoring opportunities for the guys who had the hot hand, and often, I could still finish a game in double figures because of the opportunities I created for myself. By having a sound defensive game, regardless of how my shots were falling, I was always able to walk off the floor feeling I had done my best to help my team.

I would not have had the same level of success I had at UCLA, or in the NBA ranks, had I not been exposed to John Robert Wooden. His coaching, teamwork, and achievement philosophies and motivation toward self-determination to always put forth my absolute best effort enabled me always to walk off a basketball court with my head high, regardless of the score. It was the Bruin way.

1972 NCAA Basketball Champions

VIII

BIBBY'S BUNCH

Bill and Henry made everybody's all-American teams. They finished one and two, respectively, in voting. It was the first time two players from the same team were named to the (first team) all-American teams since 1963.

Henry Bibby was the returning point guard from the 1971 championship team, so going into our first season, we were affectionately called Bibby's Bunch. Henry was a quick and heady point guard with just the right kind of persona and leadership skills to pull a bunch of underclassmen together on the floor. As the saying goes, "If you look up floor general in the dictionary, there will be a picture of Henry Bibby."

Coach Wooden was faced with replacing six of his top seven players, and most of the candidates were only sophomores. He anticipated having a good basketball team with quick fast-break talent, so we were expected to run more than UCLA had the previous year. The general public was extremely excited about the prospects for the immediate UCLA basketball future. We had ten thousand–plus people attending our preview game.

We hadn't emerged yet as the Walton Gang, but Bill Walton brought about a whole new perspective to the system. No sooner had the season began when Bill established himself as the most dominant guy in the game at the college level. His ability, superb rebounding, outstanding outlet passes, and proficient offense allowed us to do a lot more things than had we had an average, or even above-average, center. He even accelerated the level of play at UCLA and created new offensive and defensive dimensions for the Bruin attack.

For instance, as the point guard bringing the ball down court in the Wicks-Rowe era, Henry usually received the ball closer to the defensive basket. This meant that it took a little longer before he could initiate the offensive attack. Thus, the previous year's team was less of a fast-breaking threat.

With Bill, Henry was instructed to get farther down court because of Bill's strong and quick release. Bill's passes would easily beat the defense down court. All we had to do was have a man receive the ball and put it in the bucket.

Bill had a patented technique for rebounding and making the outlet pass in one movement. Bill Russell won NBA championships with his rebounding and outlet passes, and Kareem Abdul-Jabbar could snatch and kick it out with great efficiency. But you could build a game plan around the way Bill Walton got it done.

If the guard releasing were defended from getting the long outlet, the ball would go to Tommy Curtis, who was a big-time offensive threat and could pass ahead extremely well. With Tommy's ability to go to the rack and shoot well from close range, he would often draw the guy who had defended against the long outlet and then pass down low. If it were Greg Lee instead of Tommy getting the short outlet, he had the ability to pull up and hit the long jumper.

We were balanced in every little thing we did. And, with our talented personnel, we had parts that were interchangeable but could add a little twist to expose a weakness of our opponents. We were strong down low with Bill and Larry, Greg could bust the zone, and Tommy could penetrate. Then we had Hollyfield, Swen Nater, and Vince coming off the bench to cause problems. Particularly Hollyfield; he was as difficult to defend as Bill.

In our first game against the Citadel at Pauley Pavilion, Henry hit the first four shots of the game and gave us an 8–0 lead. Our full-court zone press was working to perfection. In the first three and a half minutes of the game, we got six steals. We zoomed to a 14–0 lead, and then to leads of 18–4, 24–6, 35–10, and 41–14. At the half, it was 53–27. We won 105–49. I had twelve points in my first game, and my buddy Vince had seven.

Our next game was at home against Iowa. Again, it was a blowout. We won 106–72. Henry posted thirty-two points even though he sat out almost an entire half. Larry Farmer had twenty-one, and I scored fourteen.

The next game was against Iowa State. It was a carbon copy of the previous two games, and we won 110–81. Against our next opponent, Texas A&M, we again got off to a lightening quick start. In just thirty-two seconds, we scored eight points.

The Texas A&M game was the first to offer an idea of where the team was heading as Bill hauled down eighteen rebounds while scoring twenty-three points. I had twenty-two points and seventeen rebounds. The media began to perk up, even though UCLA was already the dominant force in college basketball. Dick Enberg, the voice of the Bruins who was familiar with teams and players that comprised the UCLA dynasty, seemed to really take hold of the current edition.

By the fourth game of the season, Coach Wooden was doing all he could to hold the scores down. In his usual humble and low-key style in a newspaper interview, he finally had to admit, with a terrific but almost apologetic understatement, "I think the team is coming along faster than I anticipated."

Our next opponent was Notre Dame, who had broken a modest win streak of the Sidney-Wicks-Curtis-Rowe team, when Austin Carr went wild, scoring forty-six points to lead the Fighting Irish to an 89–82 upset victory. However, Notre Dame did not have any better luck than our previous opponents did, and we easily won 114–53.

Our average margin of victory for the first five games was 45.7 points. The secret was out of the bag: the UCLA dynasty and Coach Wooden's legacy were well intact. There was UCLA, and then there was the rest of college basketball.

We were getting ahead of teams within minutes of each tip-off with our full-court 2-2-1-zone press. The 2-2-1 was like a blowtorch! Our bench was so talented that those guys logged as much time as the starters.

Notre Dame Coach Digger Phelps was quoted as saying, "I think John Wooden could split this team, send one East, and they'd still end up playing each other in the NCAA finals."

It was well established that the second best center in college basketball was the guy playing behind Bill Walton, Swen Nater. Plus, with Vince, Hollyfield, and Gary Franklin, we had three former high-school all-Americans on the bench.

During the Notre Dame game, Henry broke the record for the consecutive number of free throws. It was a record previously set by Coach Cunningham during the 1959–1960 season when he played at UCLA for Coach Wooden. Henry hit thirty-six in a row. Coach Cunningham had thirty-four. Henry missed on what would have been number thirty-seven.

The Notre Dame game was our first big, nationally televised game. It was a coming-out event for the nation to see, and the lopsided win served notice to all of college basketball that we not only were keeping the dynasty intact but that the current edition was downright scary. Bill hit for twenty points and brought down nineteen rebounds.

More and more, Hollyfield was emerging as our big gun off the bench. Larry was a thoroughbred basketball star, and when he was in the game, the team's effort level intensified even more. We would already have a nice lead, but when Larry walked onto the court, everybody knew things were about to get even more serious. Although we played as a team, worked well as a team, and were committed to the team concept, Larry, like Bill, had his own unique swagger because he was a superior player and, in my opinion, among the top five in the country.

Our next game was against Texas Christian University. It was another avalanche, a photocopy of the others. We jumped out to a big lead and cruised to a 119–81 victory.

Only six games into our careers at UCLA, the comparisons between Bill and Kareem Abdul-Jabbar began.

Coach Wooden artfully refused to join in the comparison rhetoric, only to say that both performed well for him.

Our next game was against Texas, and it again was a carbon copy of the others, ending with a 115–65 score. It was the first time a UCLA team had won seven consecutive games by scoring over a hundred points in each.

We entered Pacific-8 conference play with an 8–0 record. After we got by Oregon State with a tough 78–72 win on the road, the rest was fairly easy. Even our games against crosstown rival Southern California weren't close. There was a lot of intensity in those games, and although USC played well, we controlled them.

USC's big star was Ron Riley, a super nice guy off the court and a hard competitor on the court. Riley and Walton really went at it and in our second game, and they had to be separated.

I also got into a shoving match with Ron after embarrassing him on a one-on-one play. On that play, I was driving to the hoop, he was defending, and we met head-on.

With the ball in my right hand, I faked a layup move to my right and then reversed for a backhand lay in. It would have been embarrassing to any defender by any offensive player. But that's not something an eighteen-year-old sophomore can do to a Division-I NCAA senior and not deal with the consequences.

A few plays later, while under the boards, I had to fend off his pugilistic retaliation. It was not as big a deal as it might have seemed to the fans or media. Those who play the game know that you have to establish your presence on the court, and in-your-face confrontations happen frequently. It's just the culture of the game and competitiveness of the individuals. When a confrontation occurs on the basketball court, a player must step to it and meet it squarely. However, he or she must also be aware that physical confrontations can lead to major personal discipline problems for the team and the school. So you have to know when to step away before emotions escalate.

We cruised into the NCAA tournament.

UCLA had won twenty-eight straight NCAA tournament games with all the previous championships. The closest team to that amount of consecutive wins was Kentucky, which won twelve straight from 1945 through 1951.

The last UCLA loss to this point was a 76–75 first-round defeat to the University of San Francisco in 1963 at Provo, Utah.

And now, there we were as Bibby's Bunch taking aim at a seventh straight title for Coach Wooden.

Bill and Henry made everybody's all-American teams. They finished one and two, respectively, in voting. It was the first time two players from the same team were named to the (first team) all-American teams since 1963, when Ron Bonham and Tom Thacker won all-American honors at the University of Cincinnati. In 1972, Sydney was a first team all-American, and Curtis Rowe was a second team all-American selection.

Others named to the all-American team that year were Jim Chones of Marquette, Ed Ratleff of Long Beach State, and Ed's high-school teammate Dwight Lamar, who was a star at Southwest Louisiana. Ed and Dwight had played together at East High in Columbus, Ohio. At Long Beach State, Ed had become one of the smoothest guards in the country, while Dwight led the country in scoring.

I was named to the Pacific-8 Second Team.

Our first tournament game was an easy 90–58 win over Weber State. Bill actually spent almost half the game on the bench, as Coach tried not to pour it on against an overmatched opponent. Two guys off the bench, Nater and Andy Hill, scored in double figures. As a team, we had sixty-five rebounds in that game, the most of any team in one game during the tournament that year.

Cal State Long Beach beat the University of San Francisco. USF's big star was Phil Smith, my future teammate at Golden State.

The two victories set up another crosstown rivalry, this time against Long Beach, a rematch between the country's number-one and number-two ranked teams. UCLA nipped Long Beach the year before in the regionals by a score of 57–55.

Long Beach was raring to get it on. They were a fast-paced entertaining team, which was a trademark of their coach Jerry Tarkanian. Their key players were returning. They had the guns, the athleticism, and, of course, a great coach. The only problem was that this was a new UCLA team with a succinctly different game. Their worst nightmare was on the horizon.

Henry lit them up with twenty-three points. Ratleff scored seventeen points, but nearly all were after the game was put away. Greg turned in a defensive gem. He held Long Beach's other guard, Chuck Terry, a future NBA veteran, to just six points. Terry played in the NBA for the Milwaukee Bucks.

Henry and Bill were named to the West Regional All-Tournament team, along with Bob Davis of Weber State, Mike Quick of San Francisco, and Ratleff.

We moved on to the Final Four and a semifinal showdown with Louisville and Coach Denny Crum, who had recruited most of the UCLA players. We dispatched Louisville 96–77 to move on to the championship match. Bill was big, with thirty-three points and twenty-one rebounds. Florida State beat North Carolina 79–75 in the other semifinal.

By now, Bill was getting labeled as the best ever. He was making people forget about UCLA greats like Fred Slaughter and Steve Patterson, and even though we hadn't completed one full year, he was drawing comparisons to Kareem.

The fan and media comparisons were like fantasy-league basketball. But there was no one in college basketball comparable to Bill, like when Elvin Hayes of Houston challenged Kareem as the best center in college basketball. So the easy comparison for fans to make was to Bill's fellow Bruin, Kareem Abdul-Jabbar.

Louisville Coach Denny Crum, who recruited Bill, cast his vote for Bill. Coach Wooden refused to feed into the fantasy comparison frenzy, only saying, "I was pleased with Kareem, or Lewis (Lew Alcindor), and I'm pleased with Walton. If you remember, Lewis did very well for us." It took Coach Wooden a few years to get away from referring to Kareem as Lew Alcindor after Kareem had embraced the Islamic religion.

The NCAA championship game proved to be our toughest challenge. Florida State had a good team and actually had an early 21–14 lead, but we got going and had a double-digit halftime lead of 50–39. They put on a long-range shooting display and defended Bill well enough to throw off our timing. In previous games, when teams tried to overplay Bill, he would still be able to move the ball and keep our rhythm going. But Florida State was successful at interrupting our pace.

We made even more adjustments at halftime. Tommy Curtis, a native of Tallahassee, Florida, where Florida State is located, started in place of Greg. Tommy proved to be the silver bullet we needed. His quick penetrations jump-started our offense, and the route was on. They actually outscored us in the second half, but the outcome was never in question, as exemplified by Coach Wooden's famous courtside calm. Coach always felt his coaching was done at the practice sessions, and when his teams hit the floor, they were well prepared to perform their best. Scenes of his famous courtside calm always show him sitting back, a rolled-up program in his hand, and his arms folded.

When they overplayed Bill, they often left me free, and I had one of my better games, finishing with twenty-three points. One of the Florida State players, Ron Harris, was quoted, "It was Wilkes who made the difference."

That game was a precursor to many more I would have in college and the NBA, playing with legendary athletes who drew a lot of attention, leaving me open to roam. Opponents would analyze the score sheet after the game and consistently see my name as top scorer. Opponents and the media made occasional references to me as the *Silent Assassin*.

Henry had eighteen points in the championship game as a crowning to his stellar career at UCLA. Although Tommy only had eight points, he was clearly the spark plug that brought high performance back to our offensive engine. Bill led our team in scoring with twenty-four points.

Bill and I were named to the all-tournament team, along with Ron King of Florida State, Bob McAdoo of North Carolina, and Jim Price of Louisville.

We finished the season 30–0, giving UCLA its sixth consecutive NCAA championship.

We had stretched the fifteen-game winning streak we inherited to forty-five. We were fifteen wins away from the all-time record of sixty set by the 1955–1957 USF teams that featured Bill Russell and K. C. Jones.

IX

THE WALTON GANG

It should be noted that the UCLA versus Notre Dame series of the 1970s is largely credited with launching the heavy televising of college basketball. It was a precursor to March Madness. Most of the big rivalries were regional. The Bruins matchup with the Fighting Irish was of national proportions and always drew big national television audiences.

During our junior year, the prospects of a ninth UCLA basketball title, seven in a row, was pretty much conceded. Certainly we had to suit up and play the games, but as long as we stayed healthy, we had the inside track.

There was more attention given to the win streak and whether we could break the University of San Francisco mark of sixty straight. We were fifteen wins away from tying the record and sixteen from breaking it.

We only lost Henry Bibby from our starting team. Our front line remained the same, with me, Larry Farmer, and, of course, the "Big Redhead" Bill Walton. Farmer had beefed up and was now twenty pounds heavier. He was not as thin as I was, but he had been a kind of wiry athletic fellow. Now he was a perfect power forward. Our first team guards to start the season were Tommy Curtis and Larry Hollyfield.

There was still enough talent on our bench. There was enough talent, in fact, for them to maybe have won a national championship of their own. There was Greg Lee, Vince Carson, Swen Nater, and Gary Franklin. As the season wore on, Greg started many games, particularly when we got to the championship tournament. There was some new talent as well: Ralph Drollinger, a seven-footer; Dave Meyers, a forward; and two guards, Pete Trgovich and Andre McCarter. McCarter soon asked to be redshirted to preserve a year of eligibility. It was a smart move. Otherwise, he would have been a fifth youthful guard on an experienced team. Next to Bill, Dave Meyers had the greatest level of intensity I've ever witnessed.

Our first game of the 1972–1973 campaign was nothing more than a continuation of the previous year. We beat Wisconsin 94–53. It was just like old times. As Humphrey Bogart says in *Casablanca*, "OK, Sam, play it again one more time." Bill had twenty-six points and twenty rebounds, I had nineteen points, and Farmer had fourteen.

As we breezed through the early games, Coach Wooden became ill with a mild heart condition. He underwent treatment at St. John's Hospital in Santa Monica and missed his first game ever in twenty-five years of coaching at UCLA. His illness was first thought to be a gastrointestinal problem.

For the players, there was a little anxiety, but everything was handled well by the athletic department. We tried not to engage in any thinking about the potential ramifications of Coach's illness. Instead, we focused on winning another conference championship. It also helped that much of our attention was on final exams.

The only game Coach missed was against the University of California at Santa Barbara. It was a 98–67 win coached by Gary Cunningham and Frank Arnold. Coach Arnold had been at UCLA for two years. He was a graduate of Idaho State. Coach's downtime was brief, and soon things were back to normal.

Nearly every article written referenced the win streak. That was the only drama to the season. As players, we never made a lot of noise about the streak, and Coach never said much about it. The streak was all media. We were all about performance on the court.

When Coach did mention it, he would ask that we not think about it and encouraged us to just go out and play our game so that, afterward, we could hold up our heads, knowing that we gave our best effort.

Our team goals were very basic and very well defined by Coach Wooden. To be successful in the eyes of the media and the fans, you had to win the NCAA championship, but the first step was by winning the Pacific-8 Conference title as a prerequisite to getting into the NCAA championship tournament.

On January 26, 1973, we tied the USF win streak of sixty games with an 87–83 win over Loyola of Chicago. It was a routine awesome Bruin performance. It seemed like we were on cruise control. Coach Wooden had always taught us to keep our emotions at an even keel. His theory was that for every mountain there is a valley. Getting up too high could be disastrous in the long run. So we always tried to be efficient, quick, and intense. In usual custom, Bill finished with thirty-two points that day, I followed with sixteen, and Hollyfield had fourteen. Hollyfield was emerging as a team leader.

Frankly, the news that day that really caught my attention more than tying the record was that Warren Spahn was elected to the Major League Baseball Hall of Fame. Mr. Spahn was one of my early baseball idols.

We broke the record against Notre Dame, the last team to have beaten UCLA, and unbeknownst to anyone at that time, the team that would stop our streak at eighty-eight.

We won at South Bend, and that was a sweet taste for Hollyfield, who was one of three players trying to stop Austin Carr two years prior in a loss to the Fighting Irish. Farmer also played in that game, and both he and Hollyfield were simply ecstatic, slapping high fives as though we had just won a national championship.

It should be noted that the UCLA versus Notre Dame series of the 1970s is largely credited with launching the heavy televising of college basketball. The Bruins matchup with the Fighting Irish was of national proportions and always drew a big television audience. It was a cross-country midseason rivalry that generated more televising of highly competitive games among top teams, and that was a precursor to March Madness, when the championship tournament grew to sixty-four teams. Up to then, most of the big rivalries were regional and, therefore, had little more than regional interest.

With UCLA being so dominant in a business-as-usual manner, the media had to really scrounge around for new angles for stories that would be more interesting than our winning.

After they wore out the comparisons between Bill and Kareem and Coach wouldn't buy into it with any controversial quotes, they asked him about other players.

Among his quotes about me were: "Our players know about Keith as much as anyone. They named him 'Silk' because he is so smooth. He does so many things, but he does them all effortlessly. In fact, many people don't appreciate him because he's like that. But, I'll tell you, the coach appreciates him." (From the *Daily Breeze*, December 27, 1973.)

"He's my type of player. He has himself under control, both physically and mentally. He never gets ruffled. He gets a lot done."

(*Los Angeles Herald-Examiner*, February 10, 1972.)

And this one was from the *Long Beach Press-Telegram*, February 15, 1973: "He's so smooth out there, he often goes unnoticed. But not by me. If you were to mold a basketball player, making exactly the kind of person you wanted, you couldn't do better than [Keith] Wilkes."

Bill Bennett, a media-relations official in the athletic and development departments for nearly half a century at UCLA, recalled that, in the same *Long Beach Press-Telegram* article written by Gary Rausch, Coach Wooden went on to give his picks for the all-time Bruin team to execute UCLA's 2-2-1 zone press. The selections were Keith Erickson, Gail Goodrich, Walt Torrence, Sidney Wicks, and myself. Coach Wooden said in the article: "He [Wilkes] would play at the number-two spot, alongside Gail and to the right of our opponent's basket. A highly intelligent player with a fine grasp of the game, he has extremely quick hands, instant reflexes, and stands tall at 6-6. So fluid is Keith in his movements that he often catches people by surprise. Many loose balls are tipped off his hands and captured by the mid-court pair."

His comments about me in the media were flattering remarks to me personally and intensified my desire to do my best for UCLA, my teammates, and Coach Wooden.

When I learned of the comment, I was pleased yet surprised. He never backed away from giving credit where credit was due, but on the other hand, the word "individual" was not among the pearls of wisdom of his Pyramid of Success. Plus, there have been many excellent players at UCLA in the Wooden years—players with terrific human characteristics and who excelled academically. I was humbled because that put me in tall cotton among names like Kareem, Wicks, Rowe, Walt Hazzard, Lucius Allen, Mike Warren, Bibby, Walton, Lynn Shackleford, Fred Slaughter, and Gail Goodrich. There were many great competitors—co-owners of the Bruin legacy—who had gone through the UCLA basketball program since Coach Wooden started there in 1948.

I could only attribute the statements to the cumulative influences of my parents, my sisters Naomi and Gail and brother Leo, Coach Swanson, and Coach Wooden himself. I reflected on what each of them meant to me and how they had helped and encouraged me. I thank God for making me that special someone to have that unique group of people in my life.

The team galloped through the conference schedule like General Sherman through Atlanta, concluding with a 76–56 win over USC. By now, Hollyfield and Bill had perfected the backdoor play. Many teams had begun to solely concentrate on Bill, and most often he would kick it to me or another outside shooter unless he found someone left alone or coming free along the baseline. Defenses could pretty much anticipate that he was going to kick the ball out once he was double-teamed.

Hollyfield was a very aggressive scoring machine. *He was one with the basket.* Once he or another guard gave the ball to Bill in the middle, Larry would slide away and then make a strong move toward the basket, kind of like a delayed give-and-go. Bill would hit him perfectly in stride with a precision bounce pass under the basket for an easy two points. By halftime of the USC game, Hollyfield had gotten the Trojans' attention by scoring twelve points.

Of course, once adjustments were made to the backdoor play, and with continued concentration on Bill, that left me open for some short jumpers. Because of Bill and Hollyfield, I went virtually unnoticed and ended up with double-figure points typical of my reputation as the *Silent Assassin*.

That game was typical of the entire season. There was no way any team could match up with us. And there was still Tommy, Farmer, Greg, Meyers, and Trgovich to contend with. We had more quickness than any team we faced, were deeper with talent, and as customary with Wooden teams, were extraordinarily poised. Were we beatable? Honestly speaking, not really. Could anybody run with us? Get real! Could they play in the half-court with us? I think not.

Having not lost a game on our shift, we opened NCAA regional play against Arizona State. Hollyfield by now was pure basketball poetry. He led us to a 98–81 walkover. The guy who had dominated the Southern California high-school scene for three years at Compton, and was a former CIF Player of the Year, was in the true form that made him a *bad dude* on the court. He scored twenty points and had six assists and five rebounds. Bill had twenty-eight points and fourteen boards.

Our next win was a 54–39 victory over USF, with Tommy having a great game, as well as Dave Meyers coming off the bench. USF tried to slow the pace and actually had a 14–9 lead, but all they had was Phil Smith, who scored seventeen points. When Tommy entered the game, he hit some long jumpers, and that forced their defense to respect the perimeter. Tommy had twelve points and four assists. Larry Farmer led our team with thirteen. Tommy made the West Regional All-Tournament Team, along with Bill. Phil Smith and Mike Quick of USF and Mike Contreras of Arizona State were also named to the team.

It was amazing that, here we were in the NCAA championship tournament featuring the best against the best, and we were still beating teams by fifteen points or more. We didn't show swagger or wear our dominance on our sleeves, but it was clear the NCAA tournament would do nothing to dispel the perception that we were invincible.

We faced Indiana in the Final Four semifinal round. Tommy was on a roll, so it didn't take long for Coach Wooden to call his number. We won 70–59, with Tommy scorching the Hoosiers for twenty-two points.

The championship game against Memphis State turned out to be one for the ages. It was a UCLA showcase. Memphis tried to guard us one-on-one and front Bill in the post. Not a good idea. Hollyfield, in his final game as a Bruin, had a two-man game going with Bill. They couldn't guard him one-on-one, and no way could they guard Bill one-on-one. Their strategy got them in deep dung. Greg Lee had an NCAA record-setting fourteen assists. He and Hollyfield (nine assists) kept lobbing the ball over the defense to Bill, who made a dazzling array of acrobatic shots. It was an instant classic and a signature game for Bill, who gave an historical record-making performance by hitting twenty-one of twenty-two shots. He had forty-four points, a record. When he wasn't scoring, he was dishing off to Hollyfield on the backdoor play. He also had thirteen rebounds. We won 87–66. I had sixteen points and seven rebounds and was the only Bruin to score double figures in all of the NCAA tournament games.

For the second year in a row, Bill was the Most Outstanding Player of the Final Four. Bill and I received first team all-American honors.

Equally important to me was that I was also selected to the Academic All-American Team.

"88 Straight"

X

EIGHTY EIGHT STRAIGHT

UCLA may be the greatest team in basketball. Not just college basketball, all basketball. If we could break their streak (seventy-six straight wins), the consequences would be greater than if we won the national championship. It would be remembered longer, because sometimes I don't think they're human."

—University of Maryland coach
Charles "Lefty" Driesell

While our junior year at UCLA was one of tremendous accomplishments, it was also a matter of good and bad news.

The good news, of course, is that we did all that we did: a second NCAA championship on our shift, number nine for UCLA, and seven in a row for Coach Wooden.

And we pushed the win streak to an amazing seventy-five games.

The intangibles that come with that kind of success, particularly for young men only months removed from being kids, were the bad news. The more attention we got, the more we withdrew.

Although Bill became very visible with anti–Vietnam War and peace demonstrations, he had no desire to capitalize on his fame and notoriety. Instead, his commitment and activity reflected his extreme sensitivity to the United States having a presence in Vietnam and other social issues where the finer ideas of humanity were in conflict with politics or super powers imposing their will by inhumane means.

In doing so, he also shattered the public expectation of him being the great white hope to compete at a position dominated by the likes of Kareem Abdul-Jabbar, Bill Russell, Wilt Chamberlain, and Willis Reed. He had the ideal Southern California image: a gifted redhead athlete from a San Diego suburb who was Mr. Basketball USA.

On the personal front, I finally got a steady girlfriend. I was milling around in front of the bookstore with some friends when I saw this attractive lady walking by. Finer than fine! Her name was Musetta, and she was from Los Angeles. She was a transfer student from Mills College in Oakland. She was wearing some cutoff jeans, had a big Afro hairstyle, and looked very intelligent yet down to earth. We started talking and later on got together to see a concert featuring Mick Jagger and the Rolling Stones and Sly and the Family Stone. We continued to date.

Other than that, I, like my teammates, was going through a period of wanting to step back from the UCLA dynasty aura. I loved basketball, my teammates, Coach Wooden, and, of course, being part of a national championship team, but it all seemed unreal. The fan adulation was much appreciated but overwhelming. It was great being popular and well received, but at no time could we be normal guys.

Every move we made in public was noticed. If we got bad service at a restaurant, we had to handle it with dignity. If we were in a hurry walking down the street and a basketball fan stopped us, we had to be gracious and engaging. We had to be careful of what we said publicly, because it was too easy for someone to misconstrue what was said as a show of arrogance.

It was hard to be humble when you actually were the best in the country and among the best in collegiate history, but it helped me in all-around personal development and prepared me well for when I had continued success in the NBA.

Everybody wanted to be our friend. And they were nice people with whom we'd want to be friends. But it was impossible to be friends with everybody or as engaging as we'd like. Moreover, there was still the number-one priority of study time. How did these people expect us to get in our study time? Some UCLA professors were sensitive to the demands of being a student-athlete, the life we chose for ourselves, but most professors only cared about classroom performance. You could not go into an economics class and tell a professor you weren't prepared for an exam because you hung out after practice.

You couldn't tell a behavior-studies professor that you were nodding off in class because you were at a late-night gathering hosted by a supporter at the Yacht Club.

On the contrary, in addition to simply wanting to do well academically, I never wanted to put a professor in a compromising position or myself in jeopardy as a result of overindulging in the hoopla. Therefore, it was necessary to make a concerted effort to pass on many of the things going on, even the opportunity to meet nice people. Taking a pass on things sometimes offended people, so I just learned to withdraw from everybody.

There was so much going in the world. Our country was finding it increasingly difficult to rationalize the Vietnam War and pulled out "with honor." Top aides to President Richard Nixon were resigning like mad as a result of the Watergate investigation. The vice president of the United States, Spiro T. Agnew, was forced to resign in the wake of a conviction of federal income-tax evasion.

There were more social issues.

The Arab-Israeli conflict was heating up in the Golan Heights. UCLA has a tremendously large international population, so international affairs like that were very topical on campus and in the classrooms. The oil crisis and a staggering stock market made our economy look vulnerable and put our future in doubt.

There were issues facing black America.

We were startled by the disclosure of the Tuskegee Experiment in which a government-sponsored program had long been using unwitting African American men in Alabama as part of a study on syphilis. Urban blight was taking hold in major cities across the country. The momentum of the civil rights movement was slowing to a crawl.

During my first three years at UCLA, I had gotten away from going to church, so basketball became my savior. But away from basketball, it was truly a mad, mad world.

Despite efforts to maintain focus on what's important in life and the goal of earning a degree at UCLA, I was still affected by all the success we had. After all, I was "Smooth As Silk" and part of an invincible team sitting on top of the world. Though I minimized public activity, I was getting comfortable with my all-American status and the celebrity that went along with it. The possibility of playing professional basketball was no longer a forbidden thought. Larry Hollyfield and Larry Farmer were drafted in the seventh round of the NBA draft (Hollyfield to Portland, Farmer three picks later to Cleveland), and Bill spurned overtures to turn pro.

I was doing well in the classroom and had my study routine down pat. I was moving into my senior year, and I knew well how to approach my class work and where to get help if needed.

College encourages thinking—using the mind. I did a lot of extracurricular reading and became interested in Eastern philosophies and religions. My interest was probably a by-product of being in an international climate like the campus of UCLA. I could see a lot of positive things about Hinduism, Buddhism, Theosophy, Transcendental Meditation, and Islam.

At the same time, Tommy, Greg, and Bill were going through a heavy Transcendental Meditation experience and were vegetarians. I gave vegetarianism a shot. It lasted three weeks. It seemed like a good thing, but I have always delighted in a good, juicy burger.

It seemed that as the notoriety pushed us inward, we were all searching for something. What clicked for me was Islam.

My personal approach was that the Supreme Being is the ultimate. It seemed that Christianity was going nuts with all the Jesus zealots (frankly speaking, before the age of verbal sensitivity, they were better known as Jesus freaks). Then there were the hippies and Yippies (Youth International Party created by Abbie Hoffman and Jerry Rubin), subcultures with a strong presence in Westwood. I probably would have shied away from that stuff even if I hadn't been conscience about needing privacy away from the basketball hoopla.

For me, Islam presented itself as the answer. I have never strayed from Christian principles. In fact, as the son of a Baptist preacher and as a local touring gospel singer in my youth, I have been and remain steeped in Christianity. But Islam has been attractive as religious study.

I enjoyed my dad's sermons, but once we gained so much notoriety in Los Angeles, I knew that going to church in Los Angeles during this introspective period would have only attracted more attention. That was something I did not want. Growing up as I did, worshipping was always a solemn thing. To me, religion has always been very personal.

I began to take the approach that, if you're living by the doctrine of your religion, you don't have to wear it on your sleeve. Of course that might have been a situational philosophy for me not going to church.

I read the *Autobiography of Malcolm X* and began to read more and more about Islam and attend services. What really attracted me was the simplicity of it during complicated times. It was an answer to my what-is-the-meaning-of-life syndrome.

A few others from the UCLA basketball program who had gone the same way did not influence my embracing Islam. Most notably were Walt (Hazzard) Abdul-Rahman and Kareem Abdul-Jabbar. I respected and admired them as men and members of the Bruins family, and, of course, I rooted for them as a true fan. But we were rarely in the same circles. A year later, after my NBA rookie season, when I told my parents I was converting to Islam, my mother freaked out. She was flat out distraught like a mother about to hear she lost her child.

My parents knew I was exploring religious philosophies, but when I told my mother I was converting to Islam, she freaked out. She was flat-out distraught, like a mother about to hear she lost her child.

"What does this mean, Sonny? Do you hate all white people?" she asked.

The Islam thing was totally new to her. She didn't differentiate the Orthodox practice from the Black Muslims practice. The Black Muslims, Nation of Islam, was the practice widely expounded upon in the fifties and sixties by Malcolm X and in the eighties and nineties by Louis Farrakhan.

It took a lot of explaining that I had nothing to do with Black Muslims or anything remotely close to a race-based practice. I'm not sure she completely understood enough to differentiate the two. Neither am I sure that I was able to put her at ease that her celebrity son had not fallen into the hands of the wrong people.

Mom's next question was, "Will you be changing your name?" My answer was yes, but I had already decided to keep my family's last name. This didn't make her feel any better. I had selected the name Jamaal, which means "inner beauty," Abdul, which means "humble servant of," and Lateef, which means "knower of the finest mysteries of subtleties," Jamaal Abdul-Lateef Wilkes.

Dad, on the other hand, did not rant and rave. Mom had enough apprehension for the whole block.

As an academic theologian and practicing pastor for decades, Dad was an authority in the various religious philosophies, and by being such an easygoing reverend, he reacted in a non-emotional, intellectual manner. However, it was clear he basically shared my mother's concern with regard to how this might affect me overall, and it was clear that he was not enchanted with the news.

I felt so intellectually and spiritually enlightened by Islam that I didn't clearly think through how they would react. I have had many intellectual, social, and spiritual conversations with my parents, and this seemed to be just another conversation and expression of my personal opinion. As older and wiser people, they were looking at this in the context of my life and my future as a family man, as well as its impact on relations with Christians. At twenty-two, I didn't have that same perspective.

I became even more isolated and totally in my own world. I was taken aback because I hadn't intended to hurt anybody. I had automatically assumed they would understand because we'd had deep conversations, and they had always been very supportive.

Nevertheless, my feelings about Islam were not swayed one iota.

In fact, I turned more inward. Islam provided me simplistic answers and the ability to put everything going on with and around me in a calm perspective.

But I was approaching everything from an idealistic level, not a realistic point. I was in search of something. I had all the time but didn't call upon Jesus Christ.

After I legally changed my name, there was a headline in the *Santa Barbara News-Press*: "Wilkes Joins Black Muslims."

The soul searching, dropping away from society, and thinking of life after college all served as distractions for the 1973–1974 team.

I don't think we were becoming complacent with winning so much, but the challenges just weren't there, and our dominance had become quite a ho-hum thing. That feeling was not reduced any by the fact that we lost Larry Farmer and Larry Hollyfield to graduation. Let's face it, when you are totally obliterating your opponents in the championships—the big dance—what's left to prove? In addition, we were getting a group of guys coming in who they were calling the best-ever class UCLA had recruited, led by a young warrior named Marques Johnson and other top national recruits Richard Washington and Jim Spillane. Marques years later would win the first John Wooden Award as the top player in college basketball.

Our campaign during my senior year began with things going on in a business-as-usual manner. We started with a 101–79 win over Arkansas. Our starting lineup now featured Bill, Tommy, David Meyers, Pete Trgovich, and me. We still had a strong second team headed by Greg, Ralph Drollinger, and Andre McCarter, who had opted for the redshirt the previous year. Most of the excitement centered around Marques, a scintillating future superstar at UCLA and later in the NBA. He had led Los Angeles Crenshaw High School to a state championship. He did not have the same credentials as Hollyfield, but he was the closest thing to that level. He may have been the top recruit in the country. Jim Spillane and Richard Washington were also freshmen and were recruited nationally.

Unlike previous years, we faced some big challenges early on in the season. Our second game was against number-eight-ranked Maryland.

Maryland Coach Charles "Lefty" Driesell had an outstanding team that included three future NBA stars: six-eleven Tom McMillen, six-nine Len Elmore, and future number-one NBA draft choice John Lucas. They were called "the UCLA of the East."

Coach Driesell wanted this game badly, even more so than a national championship.

He gave our team a lot of compliments and was quoted as saying, "You don't get an opportunity like this one very often.

"UCLA may be the greatest team in basketball. Not just college basketball, all basketball. If we could break their streak (seventy-six straight wins), the consequences would be greater than if we won the national championship. It would be remembered longer, because sometimes I don't think they're human."

He went on to say, "You know, whoever beats UCLA is going to be able to tell their grandchildren about it. Talk about the seven wonders of the world; they're the eighth."

(His words turned out to be prophetic as years have gone by, but that's getting ahead of the story.)

Coach Driesell's pregame hype to get our heads blown out of proportion almost worked. We barely escaped with a 65–64 win. We won the game on a steal by Dave Meyers, who fed to Tommy Curtis for the game-winning basket.

I think Coach Driesell's pregame hype worked best on me. I had a horrible game. I shot horribly—four for seventeen. I fouled out. I played hard, but I wasn't proud. I could have approached the game with a tougher and more competitive mentality. I did not think we could lose.

I don't think I ever disrespected anybody we played, but if I ever had, it would have been in my approach to that game. We played against a lot of great players in my first two years. Why would guys named McMillen, Elmore, and Lucas be any different? They may have been *UCLA of the East*, but we were UCLA! By the time I woke up to smell the roses, we were knee-deep in a dogfight, and I wasn't measuring up to the task. My shots weren't sinking, but my game was, and I eventually fouled out. Bill didn't do a whole lot better offensively, going eight for twenty-three shooting. But he was his usual

dominating self as chairman of the board, with twenty-
seven rebounds. He set a Pauley Pavilion record with
twenty rebounds in one half. By controlling the boards
and keeping our poise as a team, we came away with the
one-point victory and a seventy-seventh straight win.
Lefty and his UCLA of the East headed back to the land
of crab cakes. I gladly would have driven them to the
airport.

We got things back on track with our seventy-
eight consecutive win, a 77–60 victory over Southern
Methodist University. Bill pumped in twenty-five, I had
twelve, and our rising star Marques Johnson had ten.

That set the stage for a showdown with North Carolina
State.

NC State had also gone undefeated the previous
year but was barred from the NCAA tournament due to
recruiting violations in connection with a one Mr. David
Thompson. NC State also had its own notable streak of
twenty-nine straight going.

David Thompson was considered a greater collegiate
player than Oscar Robertson or Elgin Baylor.

"He can hit from anywhere inside the city limits,"
said the *Charlotte Observer*.

"He's so good, he grades ten on a scale of five," said
Tommy Heinhson, who was the Boston Celtics coach.

In Raleigh, North Carolina, where NC State is located,
they were calling the pregame week "Beat Goliath Week,"
and they were building the game up as David versus
Goliath.

Although David was a consensus all-American, he wasn't their only weapon. They also had seven-four Tom Burleson, a big forward in Tim Stoddard, and a pair of excellent guards in Mo Rivers and Monte Towe. They were coached by Norm Sloan, one of the brilliant coaches who've had great coaching success at both the collegiate and NBA levels.

It was a classic confrontation of number one versus number two.

Both teams had lost two starters from the year before, so all was even in that department. We also would be playing on a neutral site, the St. Louis Arena, before nineteen thousand people. All was even in that department as well.

Although Bill got into foul trouble, the game turned out to be just another mismatch. We won 84–66.

The headline the next day in the *Los Angeles Times* read: "UCLA's Still No.1...and N.C. State's No. 79" (the UCLA streak now stood at seventy-nine consecutive games).

And guess what? For that one game, with Bill on the bench a lot, we were dubbed the *Keith Wilkes Gang*. That's got to be the answer to a tough trivia question: "For one game, UCLA was known as the Keith Wilkes Gang; name that game."

I registered twenty-seven points against the Wolfpack, and David Meyers and Tommy Curtis also had great games. More importantly, I succeeded at the assignment of guarding David Thompson, if you considered holding one of the best-ever college basketball players to seventeen points succeeding. He took twenty shots and made seven.

Again we won. Again, things hadn't changed! At least, I didn't take them lightly, as I had the Maryland team.

David Thompson was among the best players I've ever competed against, including Julius Erving during much of my career and Michael Jordan at the end of my career, and one has to wonder where he would be among the all-time greats in all of basketball, had he not had challenging personal concerns.

Drugs were rampant in our society during the seventies, and the basketball fraternity is just a microcosm of society. It was inevitable that a percentage of players would get hung up. At UCLA, we were fortunate to have someone like John Wooden, who didn't give a lot of sermons about drugs but rather about the finer ideas of life and commitment to your endeavors and your team. Drugs simply do not have a role in your life if you are committed to being successful. I suspect there are those who disagree, and who, in fact, may have indulged as a recreation. I do not have divine authority to pass judgment on anyone's character, but it is painful to learn of anyone whose potential is shrunken to ruins because of drugs. It doesn't matter whether it's a professional athlete or someone from any other walk of life. To do so in the seventies was simply a bad idea. To do so now, in the wake of all the media attention and horror stories, is unthinkable.

After the preseason encounters with two of the top-ten teams (Maryland and NC State), there didn't appear to be much competition on the horizon in our Pacific-8 schedule. Stanford was expected to do well because they had a seven-footer in Rich Kelley, and Oregon State had a powerful and athletic freshman forward named Lonnie Shelton.

We weren't expected to face any serious challenge until our midseason game at South Bend with Notre Dame.

Meanwhile Marques Johnson was really coming along great. Correction, he was absolutely phenomenal. He was six-five, and he had been the 1973 Los Angeles City 4-A Division Player of the Year. He was fundamentally very sound and had a lot of poise—the kind of player Coach Wooden loved. It is fitting that, in 1977, he was selected as the NCAA John Wooden Award winner, the Heisman Trophy of NCAA basketball, symbolizing the country's best player in college.

His greatest assets were his amazing quickness and explosive leaping ability. He was an inch and a half shorter than me and more powerfully built but equally as quick and a much better leaper. At times he was simply low-key and efficient, a lot like my game, and at other times, he was a one-man explosion like Hollyfield. Coach Wooden, however, was more inclined to compare him to Curtis Rowe.

We headed off to South Bend to face Notre Dame, with Bill being a big question mark. He had some back problems and had sat out a couple of games prior to the trip.

At our practice session before the game, you could easily tell he was in considerable pain, because he simply could not move well in the least. But there was no way he was going to miss a big game against another top-ten opponent. At this point in the 88-straight run, every team was giving us their best shot. They were intensely focused, well prepared and giving us their "A" game with disciplined offense and gritty defense. Beating UCLA would give them a place in history and basketball folklore.

The trainers put him in a corset to help his back, and he suited up to meet Notre Dame.

Notre Dame had some great talent and was coached by the inimitable Digger Phelps. They had John Shumate, who, at six-nine, became a prototype NBA power forward. He was one of two all-American candidates. The other all-American candidate was Adrian Dantley, who was listed at six-five but was closer to six-four at best. But Adrian had a six-eleven game! They also had Bill Paterno, Gary Brokaw, and Dwight Clay. Brokaw was a very versatile player, while Clay was one of those tough, *refuse-to-lose* competitors. Clay had no fear and was nicknamed the "Iceman."

Dwight grew up in the inner city of Pittsburgh, Pennsylvania, and attended Fifth Avenue High School, which was the major rivalry to nearby school Schenley, where former NBA great Maurice Lucas attended. Growing up and going to war on a regular basis with a warrior like Maurice Lucas on the playgrounds and league competition would make life at the college level easy for anyone. Mo was a nice cat, but he was a tough hombre. He helped lead Portland to an NBA championship in 1977. He was among those who redefined the definition of power forward in the NBA, until Karl Malone of Utah came along to elevate the definition.

There was no question Bill was slightly hampered and less mobile playing with an ailing back and a corset to prevent further damage, but the game was competitive, and we actually seemed to have had things under control. But the Notre Dame crowd just would not let their team quit. They had been the last team to beat UCLA, back in 1971, when the Wicks-Rowe team went 29–1. This was a nationally televised game and the consummate inter-regional rivalry in college basketball. The Fighting Irish fans knew what was at stake. End the UCLA streak, and you're in the history books.

Ironically, it was Notre Dame's football team that was the bookends of the historical forty-seven-game winning streak of Oklahoma.

With the crowd at fever pitch, Notre Dame rolled off twelve unanswered points with four minutes left to play. They were in high gear, their fans were going berserk, and we were in a no-holds-barred, flat-out dogfight. The intensity level was through the ceiling, but basically we remained poised.

We were up 70–69 with less than a minute to play, and they wanted to get the ball into Shumate. That much we could figure out, and we shut him down. I got a bucket with forty-five seconds left in the game, but it wasn't counted. I was called for an offensive foul. But Dwight Clay, who had a running feud during the game with Tommy Curtis, got a shot off from the corner. It was a deep-corner jumper as he was falling out of bounds that made a statement, despite the fact there was more time on the clock for us to do something. There was nothing but net, and with twenty-nine seconds to go, Clay had given Notre Dame a 71–70 lead.

We had the ball with twenty-one seconds on the clock, plenty of time to regain the lead. We had five shots at the basket from Curtis, Meyers, Walton, Trgovich, and Meyers again. The ball was bouncing like a Ping-Pong ball, and it seemed like every player in uniform was in the vicinity going after the ball. I was under the basket but blocked out, despite fighting to get my hands on the ball to put up another shot. But there was no luck for anybody in a blue uniform. We had our chances— several—and we came up empty. John Shumate grabbed the last rebound, and the lights were out. The win streak had come to an end at eighty-eight.

They played a good game. They won. We maxed out— gave it everything we had. The refs let us play. There was a ton of excitement. It was a good game.

It was certainly a great game for Notre Dame , Coach Phelps and the Fighting Irish basketball team. As Maryland coach Lefty Driesell had predicted, it was a landmark game that has long been remembered. There are names in sports history that conjure instant thoughts associated with a special feat: Wilt Chamberlain's 100-point game, Henry Aaron's 714th home run, and Willis Reed's inspiring appearance in game seven of the 1970 NBA finals. From a college standpoint, add Dwight Clay to that list. His name is synonymous with the end of *eighty-eight straight*.

The Notre Dame game, in ULCA folklore, ranks right up there with the great Elvin Hayes-Lew Alcindor matchup when Elvin's Houston team had beaten UCLA in a regular-season game.

As players, we felt no shame in losing. As Coach Wooden had always asked, we gave it our best. But just like Houston, which went down to a dominating defeat in a rematch, so did Notre Dame when we faced them later and won 94–75 at Pauley. It didn't do anything for the streak, but it stopped the bleeding in terms of Notre Dame being able to get too carried away.

In between the rematch with Notre Dame, we played Santa Clara. We won 96–54. What was important was that it gave us a chance to work Marques into the starting lineup. Marques had twenty points in that game, hitting ten of eleven shots.

Then our rematch with Notre Dame came. Marques made his first start at forward, and Meyers was moved from forward to the wing position, replacing Trgovich. It was new blood in our veins. Marques was splendid, scoring with sixteen points.

The big thing about the rematch was that Bill was healed, and he scored thirty-two points, hitting sixteen of nineteen shots. It was just another day at the office as we won 94–75.

We continued to cruise through the conference, despite losing two games to Oregon and Oregon State. Marques was emerging as the new Bruin star and was definitely a crowd and media favorite. UCLA needed a Marques Johnson. Most of us had become stale. There were only so many ways for us to sum up a game, a season, our coach, or whatever. We were engaging, but we were also old news. We were overexposed locally and nationally. With Marques, the media and the fans had a new darling. He was just as talented, just as intelligent, and better-looking.

While Meyers and Marques were adding new sparks, we seniors were still out to lunch, mentally speaking, and still into that introspective bag.

Our continuous winning gave us a sense that we were frozen in time and that we were invincible. It wasn't that we felt we were too great to lose, but the matter of UCLA winning another NCAA title seemed like the natural order of things.

With three losses, we had become human and, in fact, were an up-and-down team. In the first round of the NCAA tournament, we were down. Because we were heading into the increased intensity of the NCAA Championship Tournament, we went with the experienced guys, which meant Marques did not start.

The 1974 NCAA tournament was the first tournament designated as a Division I championship. NCAA member schools previously had been divided into the University Division and College Division. The NCAA created a three-division setup, effective with the 1973–1974 academic year, by moving all of its University Division schools to Division I and splitting the College Division members into Division II (fewer scholarships) and Division III (no athletic scholarships allowed). Previous tournaments would retroactively be labeled Division I championships.

In the first game, we were extended by Johnny Davis and the Dayton Flyers, coached by Don Donoher, to a triple overtime. We won 111–100. Six Bruins, including Marques, scored in double figures. Meyers led the way with twenty-eight points. Mike Sylvester of Dayton scored a record-breaking thirty-six points, and Johnny Davis had seventeen.

We got our heads on straight long enough to get past Phil Smith and the University of San Francisco Dons, coached by Bob Gaillard. We won 83-60. I led in scoring and rebounds, with twenty-seven points and nine boards. We moved on to the Final Four.

We were matched up in the semifinal game with North Carolina State, which was coached by Norm Sloan. This time, David Thompson came to play. He had a signature game, and there was nothing or no one who was going to deny him. They had a plan, and the final touch was David. The media said he was a player who could hit from anywhere inside the city limits and could dribble on a piano. He created the concept of playing above the rim.

It was a rematch, not on neutral ground like the first game, but in North Carolina at the Greensboro Coliseum. It was yet another game we seemingly had under control but lost in double overtime, 80–77. Like the first Notre Dame game, it was another game that got away from us. Bill and I dumped in seven unanswered points in the second overtime. But the ball started bouncing their way, and they started closing the gap. Then *David* took over. I was playing aggressive defense up close on him, but he hit a jumper. We were going at it the whole game, and seconds after he canned a jumper, I got called for a foul. It was my last. I was gone. David made his free throws, then Monte Towe added a couple, and the Wolfpack's final answer to our seven-point sprint was eleven of their own.

David had done us in with twenty-eight points. He stunned us with his athleticism. While the other losses were sobering, they didn't have the finality of this one.

This was the NCAA championship, for all practical purposes. There was no tomorrow. My teammates and I were denied an eighth straight championship for Coach Wooden and another banner for the UCLA Bruins faithful.

We were slated to play in the consolation game for third place. That was something foreign to us. We were only used to winning the NCAA championship; the consolation games were for other teams. We had no interest in who was number two, three, or four. We were either number one or not. We could live with not being number one, but playing for third place had no rational basis at that level. That might have been fine for youth basketball for kids to get an extra game in, but not in the NCAA championships. We didn't want to play, and that obviously created a major national controversy. In the end, we did play, romping over Kansas 78–61.

We didn't win the championship, but we won an intellectual issue on the value of the third-place game, and the NCAA disbanded the third-place consolation game.

The NC State loss marked the end of Coach Wooden's string of NCAA titles and his string of thirty-eight straight NCAA tournament wins. North Carolina went on to win the NCAA title that year, defeating Marquette 76–64.

Bill once again was named to the All-Tournament Team that was dominated by NC State, with Monte Towe, Tom Burleson, and David. Maurice Lucas of Marquette was the fifth person.

Bill and I were named all-Americans. For the second time, I was named an academic all-American.

7511-50   The neighborhood hero, Nathaniel Cornbread Hamilton (KEITH WILKES) and
his two staunchest admirers, Earl (TIERRE TURNER) and Wilford (LARRY FISHBURNE III)
spark the action in the new American International Pictures dramatic release
"CORNBREAD, EARL AND ME," also starring Moses Gunn, Rosalind Cash, Bernie Casey.

Publicity photo for the movie "Cornbread, Earl & Me"

XI

"CORNBREAD EARL AND ME"

Never had I taken any theater-arts or acting classes, except for the history of theater arts. I had quite a bit of anxiety about how I would do and how I would fit in with those big-name actors.

J ust as we spent little time relishing in our NCAA championships, the same was the case with the North Carolina State loss.

All the guys kind of dispersed into their own thing, basically trying to graduate. Bill already had graduated with the winter class.

Although I was keeping up a good grade point average, I struggled with an economics class in my junior year. As I noted earlier, professors at UCLA are only concerned about classroom production. With this particular economics professor, I encountered a classic confrontation as a student athlete with a professor who was mindful of who played sports and hell-bent on ensuring they toed the line like any other student in class.

In my case, the professor didn't allow rescheduling a final exam due to the NCAA tournament. It was a course I needed to graduate with a degree in economics. So in my last quarter at UCLA, I repeated the course, which meant that I had to carry twenty units to graduate on time. I really did not have a lot of time to be concerned with the N.C. State game.

I graduated on time with a 3.6 grade point average on a scale of 4.0, earning a Bachelor of Science degree in economics. I also was cited among the most outstanding seniors for distinguished service to the university.

While wrapping up my degree requirements, I got a call from Coach Wooden, who was contacted by some people who had written a screenplay and wanted to know if it was a project in which I would be interested.

I returned the call. They sent me a script. I liked it and later got together with the director and writer. It was explained to me that the film required so much basketball footage that they figured it would be easier to convert a basketball player into an actor than convert an actor into a basketball player.

We read several lines a few times, and everything seemed to fall into place. They liked me, and I obviously was interested in the project.

The screenplay actually was based on a real incident in Chicago. It was about a kid who was a good student with good grades and headed to college on a full basketball scholarship. In a situation of mistaken identity, the police fatally shot the kid. In the cover-up attempt by the police to sweep the wrongful shooting under the rug, dispersions were cast upon the character of the young fellow. The project became known as the movie *Cornbread, Earl, and Me.*

I played the part of Cornbread, the kid who got shot. Tierre Turner played Earl, and Laurence Fishburne played the character *Me.*

The film featured several top African American movie stars. Bernie Casey played one of the cops involved in the shooting. The late Stack Pierce played Cornbread's dad, and Madge Sinclair played Cornbread's mom. Moses Gunn played the lawyer representing Cornbread's family. Rosalind Cash played the mother of the character Me. Antonio Vargas played the role of a hustler.

Never had I taken any theater-arts or acting classes, except for the history of theater arts. I had quite a bit of anxiety about how I would do and how I would fit in with those big-name actors. Although most of them would move on to wider national fame later in their careers, they were well known principally among African American moviegoers.

Ms. Sinclair went on to star in the hit television drama series *Trapper, John MD*, and Laurence Fishburne went on to become one of Hollywood's top box-office leading men. Mr. Pierce had numerous character roles on the big screen and a plethora of television drama programs. Casey had been an all-pro wide receiver with the Los Angeles Rams, and like Jim Brown, made a highly successful transition into the movie industry. Ms. Cash, who brings dignity and purpose to each of the roles she has played, stands as one of the elegant and gentle souls of the movie industry.

My anxiety was quickly laid to rest. Everyone treated me extremely nice, both personally and professionally. It was even more amazing that these actors had to compete against each other for movie parts that were far and few for African Americans but yet worked together like a close-knit family eagerly and kindly doing anything and everything possible to ensure the success of one and all.

They actually held my hand and helped me step-by-step along the way, particularly Madge, Rosalind, and Stack. I could never accurately explain how comforting they were to an unskilled kid in an awesome arena like the movie industry. Of course, Sidney Poitier and Billy Dee Williams never had to worry about any threat of my challenging their status as a leading box-office attraction. In fact, I couldn't see beyond the project at hand. I never had visions of becoming an honest-to-goodness actor; I simply wanted to meet the challenge and do justice to earn all of the warm graciousness and support I received from members of the cast.

The movie was released later that year. It was among a number of black films that were very popular in the mid-seventies.

After that, I had a few small parts on television programs, but *Cornbread, Earl, and Me* is the only thing the general public remembers. It's amazing how many people, non-basketball fans, would come to know me from the movie. I recall one interesting incident ten years after the film. One little girl, having recently seen the movie, was happy to see me in person because she truly had been very upset when Cornbread was killed.

XII

TURNING PRO

As a number-one pick, you are riding high, and you want to show the coach, general manager, and owner that they made a smart decision with their selection and their money. So you're psyched up, and you think you're ready. But you have no idea that there is going to be a dozen guys trying their darn best to earn recognition by kicking your butt up and down the court because you are number one!

Between satisfying graduation requirements and preparing for the movie, I had absolutely no time for anything else. This included thinking much about turning pro. Of course, back then, the financial stakes and NBA draft drama weren't what they are today.

It was pretty much a given that I'd go in the first or second round and move on to the next level, like Sydney

Wicks, Curtis Rowe, Henry Bibby, Steve Patterson, Mike Warren, Kareem Abdul-Jabbar, Lucius Allen, Lynn Shackleford, Gail Goodrich, the late Walt (Hazzard) Abdul Rahman, and Keith Erickson. All were UCLA alumni, and each was either a star player or key member of his teams in the NBA.

Conversely, there also were smaller guys who did OK as NBA forwards, like Jim McMillan and Adrian Dantley. But Larry was neither the outside shooter McMillan was nor the rebounding and put-back machine that Dantley was. Larry was just a straight-out coast-to-coast baller who had the flare of Connie Hawkins and Elgin Baylor.

I probably should have taken a note from the experiences of a handful of former Bruins who were drafted but didn't have a career in the NBA because, despite all of the great UCLA alumni in the pros, it was possible that a UCLA player could not make the grade. But the NBA draft hoopla, lottery picks, and players tagged as future franchise players before they stepped out on the court was not how things worked then. There may have been some interest as to which team I would be drafted by, but certainly no drama about getting into the pros. Bill had been the dominate college player in the mold of Bill Russell at the University of San Francisco and Kareem years earlier at UCLA, so there was little doubt about who would be the top pick and eventual Rookie of the Year.

The NBA draft took place on May 28, 1974. I was the first round draft selection of the Golden State Warriors and eleventh overall.

As a whole, big men dominated the draft. Bill was the first and went to Portland. He had graduated early and was actually already signed to them by draft time. Tom Burleson of North Carolina State was chosen second by Seattle.

Phoenix had the third pick and chose John Shumate of Notre Dame. Marvin Barnes of Providence was the fourth selection by Philadelphia.

Other first-round selections were Maurice Lucas of Marquette, who was chosen by the Chicago Bulls. Bobby Jones of North Carolina went to Houston. The Kansas City Kings drafted Scott Wedman out of Colorado. Maryland's Len Elmore went to Washington, and his teammate Tom McMillen was picked by Buffalo. Gary Brokaw of Notre Dame was the first-round pick of Milwaukee. Lucas and Jones elected to begin their professional careers in the American Basketball League.

Tommy Curtis and Greg Lee from UCLA were also drafted. Both were selected in the seventh round. Buffalo chose Tommy, and Greg went to Atlanta. It's interesting how they battled each other for four years, alternated at starting guard, positively impacted our offense with their different styles, and, in the end, were both drafted in the same round. They were quite different players but equal to each other from day one of freshman ball to the NBA draft.

At the time of my arrival to the Golden State Warriors they were an average team with a couple of stars and a roster of good players. Fans had become leery of draft picks because their more recent top picks didn't work out as expected. I didn't know a whole lot about the Warriors, but I was aware of some of their big names, like Coach Al Attles and, of course, Rick Barry, Nate Thurmond and Jeff Mullins.

Nevertheless, I was basically pretty happy to be going there. I probably would have found something good about going to any city, not to mention just having a job in the NBA, but in the Bay Area was just fine with me. It meant that I was staying on the West Coast and in California. I was born in Berkeley and had become familiar with the Bay Area while visiting my sisters Naomi at Stanford and Gail at USF.

As had always been the case when I moved on to the next level, the main topic was about my being too frail. I heard it when I went to Ventura High School and again at UCLA. I learned how to use my quickness at UCLA to defend and rebound and had been well-drilled on having a wide repertoire of shot selections. So the talk about my size, or lack of it, didn't bother me in the slightest bit.

In fact, I was more concerned about how good Golden State was. They hadn't had any luck with recent draft picks, and I began to wonder what kind of organization it was that would do so poorly with one of its most valuable assets, the draft. They had Nate Thurmond, who was in the twilight of his career ad facing the challenge of not only younger centers but also a more athletic breed. How could Thurmond, albeit a future Hall of Famer, match up on a nightly bases with guys like Kareem Abdul-Jabbar, who was dominating the league by then, Bob Lanier, Wes Unseld, Elvin Hayes, and Bill Walton in the NBA?

The Golden State rookie camp was held in July at San Jose City College. Due to the movie production and related promotional activities, I had not been training and conditioning properly. When we finished shooting,

I was off touring the country and promoting the movie. We had the movie set for release later in the year, I had met the challenge of being Cornbread, and I was riding high on being a movie star. All was well with the world. Who had time to go off conditioning when about to be a movie star?

I met Coach Al Attles right away. Al, a 1960 fifth-round pick (thirty-ninth overall) out of North Carolina A&T University, played his entire fifteen-year career with the Warriors in Philadelphia and then when the team relocated to San Francisco. He scored 6,328 points during his career and hauled in 2,463 rebounds and even more assists (2,483). His #16 jersey was retired by the Warriors organization.

Al is a big man with a big booming voice. It's the kind of voice that gets your attention, quickly.

He was immensely likeable, very down to earth, and, in his own way, a very kind and gentle person. I recall that his attire always was impeccable.

The word was that he would work your tail off. It was said that he coached the same way he played. He worked his tail off. As a player, Al didn't have dazzling athletic talents. But what he lacked athletically, he more than made up for with effort and a work ethic that is unparalleled—even still.

The most important thing you need to know about Al Attles is that he was someone with whom you did not screw around. He was nice. And to a certain point, he was tolerant. But cross his line, and he would not hesitate to put his foot knee-deep where the sun doesn't shine.

Basketball is constantly about serious testosterone among players at practice and in the games, among players and coaches, among coaches, among coaches and officials, and among players and officials. There is testosterone flying everywhere on a basketball court, and it is not the place for the faint of heart. If you are going to be a successful NBA coach, you better have bigger marbles than the next guy. Al Attles had the big marbles.

Management considered him a coach who found it difficult to discipline his guys.

Bull.

That never made any sense to me because I knew that what he wanted most was for his players to come ready to play—and ready to play hard. I'm not sure many guys in the NBA could play for Al, because he was going to get more from your abilities than you were aware you could give. Giving 100 percent or playing your best was fine in college but didn't measure up to Al's standards. You had to play by Al's definition of best effort. His definition: Hard. Hard. Hard.

The owner of the team was Franklin Meuli. He was an eccentric type who rode a Hells Angel motorcycle around town. When he wasn't riding his bike, he was in his Corvette. He also spent a lot of time on his yacht, cruising on the Pacific Ocean. I didn't see him a lot, which was OK with me. He wasn't around very much and let General Manager Dick Vertlieb handle the team.

At rookie camp, it seemed all eyes were on me. I was the number-one draft choice, and I was a heralded two-time all-American from the John Wooden dynasty at UCLA.

In addition to the rookies selected in the draft, there were some free agents at rookie camp. In all, there were a dozen players.

The guy who started making his presence known right away was Frank Kendrick, a six-six forward who was selected in the third round out of Purdue University. Frank could play, and he had a dominant court presence. He was the man in camp. He was brilliant inside or on the perimeter. And he was talking trash all the while. We used to kid him a lot about his little hands and feet. But he was dominating on the court.

As a third-round draft choice, there was a lot more pressure for him to perform well, and Frank rose to the occasion. It seemed a certainty he was going to make the team.

It also was obvious that Phil Smith would make the club. Phil was the second-round selection out of the University of San Francisco. He was an excellent athlete who later became one of the premier guards in the NBA.

I kind of thought I'd be sticking around too, particularly since I already was signed to a deal. However, I was not mentally prepared for everybody in camp coming at me so aggressively. It was kind of like an old western movie, where gunslingers came from throughout the West to have a showdown with the fast gun.

It seemed that everyone's main objective was to outshine the number-one pick. That would be me! The mind-set of the guys in camp was:

If you don't do anything else in camp, go hard against the number one pick and see what happens.

Get in his face. Block his shot. Don't let him shoot. Box him out. Deny him the ball. Go to the hole or shoot the jumper whenever he comes near. Bump and grind with him, maybe the coaches will take notice of how tough you are

Leap stronger and higher for rebounds when he's around the boards. Make strong cuts and backdoor moves when he's defending you. Let them see how hard you make him work. Do whatever you can and have to do to make the team, but do it against the fast gun, because he's the center of attention.

Don't waste as much time and energy going hard against other rookies or free agents, because they aren't the top prospect. Do it against the guy who they're betting on to be NBA material, and let's see what happens. Outshine him, and you've got a good chance at winning a job.

You can't blame the players for having that mentality because it's worth the effort. It's worth an extra effort.

The difference between making the team and getting cut is huge. The motivation is definitely there; all you have to do is do your best, against the top draft pick. Go hard, and let's see what happens.

It was immediately clear to me why first-round draft selections often do not pan out. As the number-one pick, you are feeling good about yourself, and you want to show the coach, general manager, and owner they made a smart decision with their selection and money. So you're psyched up, and you *think* you're ready. But you have no idea that there is going to be a dozen guys trying their darn best to earn recognition by kicking your butt up and down the court because you are number one.

That wasn't the only problem I had.

About the third day of camp, I cramped up during practice. I hyperventilated, scaring everybody to death. They had to carry me off the court and into the locker room to ice me down. Rookie camp for me was over. I had to sit on the sidelines and watch the rest of the way.

Despite the stress of dealing with all the aggressiveness coming from each and every player in every drill and every scrimmage, I wanted to step up to the challenge. I figured that once I'd sized up the enemy, I would have the answer to whatever they were throwing down. I didn't doubt myself, but I was now on the sidelines and unable to step to the challenges.

Maybe all the aggressiveness got to me and wore me down? Maybe the time spent on promoting the movie and not getting mentally and physically tough enough for camp was the issue? Whatever it was, I stunk up the place! And I knew it.

Whatever excuse I could come up with, the bottom
line was that I was not physically and mentally prepared,
and it glowed like a neon sign in Manhattan. I bombed
out at rookie camp. Furthermore, I was well aware of
the consequences of going to camp when not in tip-top
shape. I wasn't aware of how humbling it would actually
feel. Nobody and nothing could have saved me – not
Bob Swanson, not John Wooden, not any all-American
honor, and not any of those NCAA championships. For
the first time in my life, I was not a favorite son, and I
was falling on my face.

Mr. *Smooth As Silk* had turned into lumpy oatmeal.
If I didn't make some giant strides to turn my situation
around, the brightest future for me at that point, well,
wasn't very bright at all. If I was to turn this ship around,
I was going to have to *bring it* on the very next chance I
got.

Going up against "The Big E" Elvin Hayes

XIII

ROOKIE OF THE YEAR

Elvin Hayes took me apart. He simply used and abused me. With my head hung down, I exited the locker room, and just ahead of me was the Big E. He was talking with some people in the corridor. He stopped his conversation and came over to me and said, "Hey, you're a young boy. You're going to have nights like that. Don't worry about the slump. You're going to play a long time in this league. Good luck to you."

Rookie camp was a total embarrassment. When I got back home in the Los Angeles area, I made a commitment to get to work and get in shape. The guys at rookie camp had themselves a big laugh, and most had a good showing—at my expense.

I was determined to use the experience to my advantage. This was now about pride and redemption. I was motivated beyond making the Golden State Warriors roster. This had become personal. I was representing my coaches and teammates from the Ventura youth basketball league, Ventura High School, Santa Barbara High School, and UCLA. I had to summon everything within me: the precision and efficiency I learned, the many years that Coach Swanson put in with me, the precision and efficiency I learned from Coach Wooden at UCLA, and the poise and confidence from being part of the Bruins dynasty. My work was cut out for me.

I labored with tunnel vision and intensity. A repeat performance of my showing in rookie camp was not an option. No one had to tell me what to do or how important it was. I defined my purpose, I defined my work ethic, and I defined my commitment. My definitions and expectations were greater and more intense than that of anybody else.

Basketball was only a part of my workout program. There was extensive running to build my legs and endurance. I engaged an aerobics component to ensure that all parts of my body, from the top of my head to the tip of my toes, would be in top athletic condition. I enrolled in a martial-arts program in Van Nuys, just over the hill from UCLA.

I didn't worry about how physical the NBA was going to be. The NBA—Warriors, in particular—needed to worry about how physical I was going to be.

I was prepared to get physical to the point of scrapping with all comers if I had to in order to establish myself. It was abundantly clear in rookie camp that the mental toughness was a whole new ball game, and if I were going to be successful, I would have to man-up to the NBA level. Not that they were tough guys or pugilistic, but the level of play was extremely aggressive at every move, with or without the ball. But on the other hand, if you are going to be aggressive, you'd better be prepared for anything. The Warriors rookies and free agents had emphatically shown me that they came to play. Now it was my call to raise the table stakes. I was on a mission, and it felt good.

Over the summer, the Warriors traded Nate Thurmond to the Chicago Bulls in exchange for Clifford Ray. This was a major move by the organization, because Nate was an institution in the Bay Area. He was a team leader and a civic leader. Even to this day, Nate is an institution in the San Francisco Bay Area.

The outlook for the season was filled with question marks. The Warriors had lost Cazzie Russell, a prolific scorer, and Thurmond, a veteran all-star center.

I arrived in the Bay Area prior to the opening of camp so that I could get an apartment and put my personal affairs in order.

George Johnson, a center with the Warriors out of Dillard University in New Orleans, and his wife Dee made sure I knew my way around. Dee also made sure that I had some good home-cooked food.

There were some informal practices being held at a recreation center in San Bruno. That is where I first met Rick Barry.

The moment I saw his game, I started looking forward to playing with him. I remember watching him play for a while before I got onto the court. Rick was pure basketball poetry, and he was just going through the motions.

He greeted me cordially. At the same time, it didn't take long to know whose show it was going to be at Golden State.

Although Rick was cordial, he was very much to the point. He was not curt in any way, but definitely to the point. The early impression I got was that he was a person who liked to keep his distance. In retrospect, I understand more clearly what his early thoughts may have been. The Warriors had taken on a new complexion, and there was a lot to find out before people could have the luxury of being personable. Although a veteran lineup was penciled in as the starters, no one really knew what to expect when camp opened up at San Jose City College.

The starting guards were Charlie "CJ" Johnson and Alfred "Butch" Beard. CJ was the star at the University of California when I had thought about going to college there. Butch was the quarterback of the team. Derek Dickey was slated to start opposite of Rick, and George Johnson was the center.

We worked out twice a day. This was new to me since I had only played ball in school, and practices were held during the course of the school year. We did a lot of running, and practices were very grueling.

At the pro level, basketball is your job. Whatever else you got going on, except God and your family, is secondary. So there is no concern about time. You are no longer a student athlete. You are a professional athlete. As a result, the proficiency of a two-hour practice that you were accustomed to in school, or even in recreation ball, is a thing of the past.

There was lot to learn about the pros, and not just the Golden State offensive and defensive systems.

Certain guys in the NBA had established styles of playing that included tricks of the trade that would be considered fouls by everyone else but were strategies that only they could get away with. You had to learn how to play against them with knowledge of their tendencies, what their tricks were, and what kinds of things the refs would let them get away with.

For instance, John Havlicek would slap your hand to make a steal but would never get called on it. *Or rarely ever* if he did get called. It's something I was later able to do and frequently get away with after I became an established player. That's what is known as your playing identity.

The new guys on the team were working hard to establish their game and show what they could do, while the veterans didn't get serious until late in the exhibition season.

The number-one thing with Al was that guys showed up ready to play and play hard. I already had one strike against me because I hadn't put in a full rookie camp. He got my total cooperation, and I blocked out everything else in the world. The team, as a whole, understood what Al demanded, and we conducted ourselves accordingly. We appreciated a coach who demanded the absolute most of out of us, and we were prepared to go to the end of the earth for him.

Our team featured a great center duo, with Clifford Ray being the power guy, and George being the finesse type. Rick and Clifford ran the pick-and-roll to perfection, and George would often shut down the lane with his shot blocking in the fourth quarter.

Butch always played the toughest opposing guard, as well as running the point. CJ was a jumping jack who could make the big defensive play. Having played collegiate ball in the Bay Area, CJ was immensely popular and a man who enjoyed being a bachelor. He drove a classic Jaguar that everybody marveled at. The spotlight of the Warriors was Rick's scoring and passing abilities.

Guys easily picked up nicknames. We called Clifford "Yo Hon." Clifford was a very colorful person (and has remained one of my closest friends). He was a gourmet cook and a classical musician.

Every time Clifford would see a pretty woman, and I mean every time, he'd holler out, "You! Yo, hon." He had a big sense of humor, which was a big asset in some tense situations.

We called George "Nupes," which was derived from his college fraternity, Kappa Alpha Psi, at Dillard University in New Orleans.

Charles Dudley was a reserve guard we called "Hopper." It was a name from the "Kung Fu" television series in which David Carradine was referred to in his youth as "Grasshopper" by his wise sensei.

In practice, Dudley was a tough player who would literally beat the stuffing out of a man. That earned him the name *Hopper*.

Derek Dickey was a well-built athlete and very well liked. He had an affinity for exotic snakes. We're talking about boa constrictors and pythons. He was a model family man who really loved his kids.

Phil Smith was a huge favorite at camp. Like CJ, he was a big local sports hero, having had a great career at USF.

Frank Kendrick made the team. However, he was later released when the Warriors were able to pick Bill Bridges for the stretch drive toward the play-offs.

And then there was the man affectionately called "Ricky Pooh"—Rick Barry!

He was the main man. He had the reputation and the game to match. He was our marquee player. He had been a legendary scoring machine in his own time in the ABA and had jumped leagues to the NBA. He had a prima-donna reputation. He was a perfectionist. But Rick was a personable guy and was a student of intricacies of the game, loved the game, and knew how to exploit an opponent.

We jokingly said that Rick would have made a great lawyer because he would always argue. He seemingly would argue about the time of day, and for no apparent reason. Most guys argue to some degree, but most will shout or mumble their thoughts as they are walking away and moving on. Rick most often had a case to make, and usually it was about something technical or something that should be fundamentally understood.

Most perfectionists are taken aback, if not flat-out befuddled, when a player, ref, or coach does something that doesn't fall in order. That's kind of how Rick was. He knew the rules, he knew how the game was supposed to be played, and he would share his knowledge if there were a need to do so.

We were picked to finish fourth in the Pacific Division that year. But this was a team of guys with a lot to prove.

I had played in the shadow of Bill Walton as part of the Walton Gang. This was my opportunity to show what I could do on my own. Phil had been a star in the area already, and he had a celebrated sports status to build upon. Rick and Clifford were seasoned pros but hadn't won the big one, an NBA Championship.

We got out of the gate just like the UCLA Bruins teams. We won ten straight. I came off the bench for the first seven games. I was playing about half the game. Then Derek pulled a hamstring, and I started in his place. I stayed there when he returned.

The alternating of Derek and I worked in a constructive manner, like George and Clifford. When Derek came back, he still played a lot. We continued to split the time evenly, just as we had been doing when he started. He was still getting a lot of media attention and fan appreciation.

I found irony in my current status. I was said to be too frail to play in the NBA, and there were a ton of questions about my durability. Yet there I was starting at the power-forward position in my rookie season with the best team in basketball. Each game I was playing against the opposing power forward, and I was doing a little bruising of my own while scoring in double figures and getting double-figure rebounds.

The success was directly attributable to the UCLA program in which fundamentals were second nature. It was there that I gained knowledge of angular relationships on the court and, of course, the all-important matter of blocking out.

It was from Coach Wooden and Coach Swanson at Ventura that my fundamentals were developed, like creating space. Even if you can't jump, even if you can't manipulate your way to box out, you can always out-quick someone once you've created space. That's why Coach Wooden, and his number-one disciple Denny Crum, always recruited quick players.

It was those fundamentals that enabled me to perform well at power forward, much to the surprise of just about everyone. Fundamentals helped me compensate for my smaller frame and outplay taller and heavier power forwards. I also had an additional plus factor: Clifford Ray!

Clifford was a prototype power center. He helped me develop a formidable inside game, further utilizing my quickness and fundamentals. Although I knew how to play inside and was fundamentally sound, more so than many opponents, I actually did not have an *inside game* that was my trademark until Clifford tutored me.

By midseason, I had arrived in the NBA. I was there, I was starting, and I was on one of the league's top teams—at power forward! We were winning. So far, nothing had changed.

Then it happened. A slump!

I hit a slump in the middle of the year, just when I had gained a lot of confidence. We're talking about a rock-bottom slump.

I'm sure Al wanted to take me of out of the starting lineup, but he probably didn't want to undo something he had done by making me a starter in the first place and keeping me there when Derek returned. With the fragile psyche of a young rookie, had he taken me out, my confidence that he had worked hard to build might have evaporated.

I was far down the skids when we played against the Washington Bullets in a home game one evening.

Elvin Hayes took me apart. He simply used and abused me. With my head hung down, I exited the locker room, and just ahead of me was the Big E. He was talking with some people in the corridor. He stopped his conversation and came over to me and said, "Hey, you're a young rookie. You're going to have nights like that. Don't worry about the slump. You're going to play a long time in this league. Good luck to you."

His going out of his way to say something like that to me made a big impression. I was really, really down, and his words alone perked me back up.

When you're slumping in the NBA, playing night-in and night out, you start feeling like you can't do anything. You're listless for days on end. But yet, you must suck it up and go back out there, because you are a professional. Eventually, I began to come back around to being a contributor to the Warriors.

The way Al Attles handled what was truly an awful situation and the way Elvin stepped forward to uplift the troubled soul of a rookie kid he didn't personally know are the things that make those two fellows unique individuals. Those are the things that will never be reflected in the career highlights of Al as a championship coach or Elvin as one of the greatest ever to play the game, but they are the things that reinforce our belief in the goodness of mankind.

About midyear, I got to know a completely different side of Rick Barry. For the first few months, our relationship was strictly professional. Rick spearheaded a Christmas drive for one of the local predominately black Catholic high schools. He personally made sure that some of the guys on the team got involved in the project.

I was one of the guys, at Rick's urging, to get involved. It was during this time that I also got to meet his family, and I got to know him off and away from the court.

We became good friends, and began a journey into a lasting friendship to this day. I started learning more about the game from him.

He taught me a lot about creating scoring opportunities. Much of it was a lot like what Wooden and Swanson taught, but this was finishing school! And there was no one better on God's earth, who was better for me as a personal tutor in scoring, than Rick Barry. We were of similar size and stature and had the same type of offensive game. This was a finishing school that took my offensive game to a new level.

For instance, one move he taught me was the rocker step. Another was setting up the crossover move. Both are offensive pivot steps to create space between the scorer and the defender. Rick was a master scorer. I enjoyed watching him in games and as practice. Even though he was a teammate and we were both professional men in the NBA, he became my idol. I began envisioning myself as the heir apparent, the next Rick Barry, to succeed him as the scoring leader of the Warriors.

Elgin Baylor and Jerry West were childhood idols from a distance via radio and television highlights. Rick was an idol right up front and personal.

I became a disciple of his determination to win. In college, you kind of followed the tempo set by the coaches. At the pro level, it's about what you bring to the party. Determination to make the grade is a major element. Determination to win is yet another element. And that's where Rick Barry was. He was on yet another level from most players.

As a perfectionist, he was harder on himself as he might have been on other people. Once I got to know him, I understood that he was simply a competitor and a motivator.

Another thing about Rick was that he had somewhat of an offbeat sense of humor. One guy would get on you to be funny, and you understood the humor. A lot of times, when Rick got on you, his expression or way of saying something didn't match up with the fact that he actually was trying to be funny. Plus, it was *Rick Barry* getting on you.

His offbeat humor, combined with his perfectionism, led some people to read him wrong—even to the point of leaving one flat-footed of whether or not he was joking about something. But on the floor, he was a driven person who didn't give an inch. Not even to himself.

With the success we were having, management made a commitment to go all the way. They waived Frank Kendrick and picked up Bill Bridges, the great forward from the University of Kansas who recorded a double-double over his NBA career, averaging 11.9 points and 11.9 rebounds per game.

In play-off competition, you cannot possibly have too much of the kind of rebounding experience and muscle that Bridges could provide.

We won the division by seven games. No one thought we could do that. In fact, the Oakland coliseum, *where we called home*, was booked for ice-skating shows during the time period of the NBA championship series.

Nevertheless, the town was going crazy. The other pro teams in town, the Raiders and the Oakland A's, were winning big. And now, so were their Warriors. It was becoming the proverbial city of champions. It was just a wild and crazy time for the fans.

Dick Vertlieb, the general manager, was a real grass-roots kind of promoter. Hal Childs was the director of public relations. They both loved the game and enjoyed their professions. They were enthusiastic guys whose presence added some adventuresome spirit to the mix of characters on the court. The legendary Bill King was the voice of the Warriors and he was a very highly respected and colorful broadcaster.

One day after practice before the play-offs began Dick came into the locker room with a briefcase. He offered congratulations to us for winning the division. And then he opened up the briefcase. In it was twenty-five thousand dollars in small bills. Then he said, "I just wanted you guys to see what twenty-five thousand dollars looks like." That was in reference to each player's share if we could win the NBA championship.

We ended the regular season with a .588 winning
percentage. Our winning the division and having the
best record in the conference earned us a bye for the first
round of the play-offs.

It had been a phenomenal year for Rick, and he was
ready to carry it over into the play-offs. He had scored
thirty or more points in forty-six games during the season
and forty or more points fifteen times. His season high
was a fifty-five-point game against Philadelphia. Rick led
the team in scoring, of course, but check this out: he also
led the team in assists and steals!

I took particular note of the fact that he led in assists
and steals by wide margins. He had 492 assists, Butch
Beard, the point guard and closest leader to him, had 345.
Rick had 228 steals. The closest to him in that department
was Charlie Johnson with 138, and Butch had 132.

I was en route to earning NBA Rookie of the year
honors, finishing second on the team in scoring and
rebounding, and I was fourth in assists. Clifford led the
team in rebounding with 870 boards.

Winning Rookie of the Year honors was an especially
sweet redemption for my pitiful rookie-camp experience
and midseason slump. It also was rewarding because one
of the other top rookies was Bill Walton, my friend and
former teammate at UCLA, who had been the number-one
overall pick and to whom the Rookie of the Year award was
conceded at the beginning of the year, and rightfully so.

Most importantly, it was sweet because of all
the questions about whether I could withstand the
punishment of the inside game at the NBA level. And I

had done so at the power-forward position after having been drafted eleventh overall, behind a host of other big men.

As for the rookie-camp experience, I could safely exhale and even laugh about it.

We had a nine-day hiatus before our first game. We were well rested when we began play-off competition against the Seattle Supersonics.

The Supersonics team was coached by Hall of Famer Bill Russell and was a great team. They had an awesome inside game, with Tom Burleson, Spencer Haywood, and Leonard Gray. They had size and talent that posed a serious challenge to us and solid guards in Archie Clark, Donald Earl "Slick" Watts, and Fred "Downtown" Brown.

At this point in the series, we were hitting on all cylinders, and we knew where our meal ticket was. We won my first-ever play-off game 123–96. Actually, I got off to a bad start, but nothing really mattered, because Rick was shooting the lights out like a man possessed. The series seesawed, and momentum swung back and forth. We won game five by another big margin, 124–100. Then we put them away in the sixth game with a 105–96 win. In the finale, Rick had thirty-one points, and I chipped in with twenty.

I was scoring a little above my season average. This was a good thing, because our next series was against the Chicago Bulls for the Western Conference Championship. I never kept a line on betting, but I believe Chicago might have been favored. Our only hope was that the schedule favored us, and, of course, we had Mr. Rick Barry.

The Bulls, coached by Dick Motta, may very well have had their best team ever to that point in their history. They had guys with whom you'd like to go to war today. They included Bob "Butterbean" Love, who you didn't want to leave alone in the corner or on the perimeter; crafty veterans in Chet Walker, Jerry Sloan, and Matt Goukas; a hard-nosed pesky guard in Norm VanLier; and Nate Thurmond at center.

We got out of the blocks OK with a 107–89 win. But they came back with a one-point victory in the second game, winning 90–89.

They rocked us in the third game, with Norm scoring thirty-five points while playing the entire game. They went up in the series, two games to one. We seesawed over the next couple of games and entered game six with our backs to the wall in Chicago.

Once again, it was Rick who rose to the occasion with thirty-six points, leading us to an 86–72 low-scoring victory.

In game seven, the Bulls had a very dominating defense in the first half. They had both Rick and myself bottled up.

On offense, they would take as much air out of the ball as possible by using as much time as possible off the twenty-four-second clock. We were down by as many as fourteen points in the second quarter.

The second half didn't look much better. Rick got into foul trouble. With Rick on the bench most of the third quarter, I became the first scoring option and responded with ten points. That helped pull us within six. Once Rick got back into the game, we caught them and put them away 83–79. I finished with twenty-three points, and Rick had twenty-two.

That was a big game for us, because it showed that we had another legitimate scoring option besides Rick Barry: his mentee. To that point, we had a good team with guys who could bring it, but only one go-to guy. I think Rick was pleased most of all that we came through and relieved him of some of the pressure.

We advanced to the NBA finals to face the Washington Bullets. The stage was set for one of the miracle upsets in NBA finals history.

The Washington Bullets and Boston Celtics were the class of the NBA and were battling it out for the Eastern Conference Championship. It was often said the East Coast was where you would find the blue bloods of basketball, particularly New York, Philadelphia, Boston, Detroit, Baltimore, and Washington, DC, as well as Chicago in the Midwest. From the playgrounds (with guys like Albert and Bernard King, Earl Manigault, and Connie Hawkins) to the pros (with guys like Earl "The Pearl" Monroe, Bill Russell, John Havlicek, Walt Frazier, Julius Erving, and Wes Unseld), if you had an *East Coast rep*, you were legit. Even guys like Wilt Chamberlain, Kareem Abdul-Jabbar, Kobe Bryant, and Lamar Odom (who all had the spotlight on the West Coast at one time or another) first earned their reputations on the East Coast, and each was considered legit before ever setting foot on the West Coast. Conversely, going from the West to the East Coast, you had to be tested East-Coast style, even if you had a West Coast rep.

Coming from the laid-back West Coast, we were going into the eye of the storm. We won our regular season conference convincingly, but we were only fourteen games over .500. The Bullets and Celtics had played well over .700 ball. They went the distance like two heavyweights in the conference finals, and Washington won. Now the only thing that stood in the way of a certain NBA title for the Bullets was a featherweight: the Golden State Warriors—or so it seemed.

The Bullets finished were coached by K.C. Jones and had beaten his old Boston Celtics team in the Eastern Conference finals. Washington was loaded with great talent. They had Wes Unseld and Elvin "the Big E" Hayes, and that alone was enough to strike fear in most opponents, but they also had the versatile Phil Chenier and hard-nosed ballers in Mike Riordin and Kevin Porter.

In the first game at Washington, the Big E and his boys did what was expected. They brought it to us, big time. They rolled up a 54–40 halftime lead and went up by as many as sixteen points in the third quarter. The writing was on the wall, but Al Attles wasn't having it! He was going to get as much out of us on the last day of the season as he had gotten out of us on the first day of practice: more than we thought we had to give. Al had an *East Coast rep* of his own growing up in New Jersey, playing college ball at North Carolina A&T, and starting his career with the then Philadelphia Warriors as a protégé to Chamberlain. To him, it wasn't a matter of how big you were but how *bad* you were.

Rick and I both were having an off night. Charles Dudley and Derek Dickey were carrying the load on offense. Clifford Ray was a monster on the boards. Against all odds going into the game, and having an uphill battle throughout most of the game, we came away with a 101–95 win.

Clifford pulled down sixteen rebounds. I only had ten points, but I chipped in with thirteen rebounds and helped cool off the Big E in the second half. That game must have been an omen of things to come.

In the second game, the Bullets again led at the half, this time by six points. But in this game, *the Rick was on.* He had the hot hand, and he and Phil Chenier had a shoot-out. Phil learned, like everyone else in the NBA, that the opponent more often than not will lose in a shoot-out with Rick Barry. Phil gallantly put up thirty; Rick notched thirty-six.

More importantly, Golden State had ninety-six, and Washington had ninety-five. We also had two games in the win column. The big bad wolf, Washington, had none.

And guess what? *We were headed home.*

Since our home court, the Oakland Coliseum, was booked for ice-skating, we played at the Cow Palace in San Francisco.

The Bullets came to town determined to get things back on track. They were the blue bloods. They had the most outstanding regular season. It was the natural order of things. But by now, Rick was on fire. He was at his NBA best. He put on a clinic in game three. He scored thirty-eight points. He had that picturesque jumper going, as well as textbook drives to the bucket. If ever there was a single-handed win, it was that one. We prevailed again, 109–101, and went up three–zip.

By now, NBA fans across the country were amazed, and Golden State fans were euphoric.

We were a good team; Washington was a great team. We played in a weak conference; Washington played in a tough conference.

We were one-dimensional with Rick Barry, while they had a strong inside scoring duo in Unseld and Hayes, and they arguably had the best pair of guards in the league in Porter and Chenier. But we had Al Attles and Rick Barry and were on the verge of a sweep, and the Bullets were looking at an oncoming train.

Game four hadn't been long started when Rick was the victim of a foul by Mike Riordin, which Al argued was excessively hard and deliberate.

Al became vehement in voicing his objection. If you know basketball, you would know it was intentional. Besides, Mike Riordin was one of the headiest players. He wasn't going to get into that kind of fouling early on unless he was sending a message.

Now hear this, Al is the absolute last person on earth you would want to see fighting mad. He went off the deep end. He had to be restrained from jumping on Riordin. He was ejected from the game.

They were going after Rick to get him riled up and out of the game. They did even better; they got the coach. From a Washington viewpoint, it was a great strategy. Their backs were against the wall, so anything went.

The Bullets continued to frustrate Rick. They were trying their darn best to tie him up. They had one guy in his face and another in his jock. It was a game fought tooth and nail.

As was the pattern throughout the series, they had the upper hand most of the way. They were leading late in the fourth quarter, 92–88.

I hit a twenty-foot jumper to bring us within two at 92–90. It was one of my patented jumpers that later was dubbed the twenty-foot layup. Then I scrapped my way between Unseld and Hayes, two of the best rebounders in the history of the game, to get an offensive rebound and score with an inside bucket. That tied the game at ninety-two, and the die was cast. We went on to win it 96–95.

It was the first of my four NBA championships, and the first of seven NBA championship finals series.

I now had traveled the whole nine. I had given up baseball as a kid to play basketball. I did well enough to earn a scholarship to UCLA. I had won all-American and academic all-American honors twice at UCLA, along with two NCAA championships under John Wooden.

Now I could add an NBA championship and the honor of being the NBA Rookie of the Year. Life was good.

My first order of business after the season was to sit down with Warriors management and my representatives to review my contract and their verbal commitment. It had not gotten past me that they had said they would increase the numbers and extend the life of the contract if I made it in the NBA. But it did slip past everybody else. Nobody else remembered the promise! Not even my representatives. I was crushed. But it was my most important business lesson. *Get it in writing.*

NBA championships or whatever, I became extremely disenchanted about staying with the Warriors for two years, knowing that I was grossly underpaid relative to my role in the championship season and my personal accomplishments. They reneged on a promise. I knew, and God knew it. It mattered not how everyone else played his or her hand in the matter.

I seriously contemplated getting out of basketball; that's how crushed I was. I was absolutely astonished that people could make a promise, renege, and lie about it. I thought very seriously about going to law school. If this was business in the NBA, you can have it.

As angry as I was with Golden State for reneging on their oral promise to renegotiate after my successful rookie season, I had mixed feelings. I knew the people, the system, and enjoyed living in the area. I had been told it could be my team and had been looking at houses in the area. It was a time when the NBA was transitioning from a rich-man's hobby to a big corporate business, and I believe Franklin Meuli simply did not have the resources to keep me or a number of other players the Warriors lost.

Eventually, of course, I collected myself and realized that all things considered, I was in a good position.

I had been successful enough my first year, and indications were that I could have a good career in basketball if I persevered through the Warriors situation. So in the interest of not killing off a promising career, I bit the bullet and returned.

Following the playoffs, in the first round of the daft, we selected a highly talented forward-center out of LaSalle College by the name of Joe Bryant, the father of Kobe Bryant. He was traded to his hometown team of Philadelphia, however, and never became a teammate. I went head-to-head and toe-to-toe with Joe a few times, and many times I saw the same flash and skill that the world would later see in his son. In the second round, we drafted an old nemesis of mine, Gus Williams from USC. Gus was a great addition to the team. He learned the NBA game under the tutelage of Phil Smith and Charlie Johnson but, after a couple of years, left for Seattle, where he became one of the best guards in the NBA during his tenure.

We made the play-offs the following two years. Phoenix dethroned us in the conference championship series, and the following year, the Los Angeles Lakers knocked us off. That was my option year, and when the horn sounded at the end of my final Warriors game against the Lakers, I was a free agent.

I was an established pro, one of the NBA's top forwards at both ends of the court, and I was walking away from Golden State without giving them the possibility of a conversation.

Maybe what happened was just the way they do business, but it was of no consequence to me because I was free, happy, and marketable.

XIV

DR. J MAKES A HOUSE CALL

David was a player in the mold of Dr. J, Michael Jordan, and Kobe Bryant, but at six-four, he was a tad shorter, which made his gravity-defying feats even more entertaining. He had a forty-four-inch vertical leap and was called The Sky-walker. His legend extends to the proportions of Earl Manigault, "The Goat" of New York, as it is said both could snag money from the top of the backboard and leave change.

After the Warriors 1974–1975 championship season, we were propositioned by the Kentucky Colonels of the American Basketball Association to compete in a World Series of Basketball, with a one-million-dollar purse.

Like the American Football League had done to force a merger with the National Football League and subsequent big ticket Super Bowl, the ABA was knocking on the door to bring about higher visibility and profits for their league.

Unfortunately, such a game was impractical from the standpoint of the length of the season and players needing to get in some vacation time before camp opened up. We would all have enjoyed a Super Bowl like payday, but an NBA versus ABA championship showdown would need to have been properly planned and promoted to maximize its full potential and revenues.

The ABA had shown it could compete with NBA teams. Interleague play had begun in 1971, and after that first year, the ABA not only held its own, but had an advantage.

Obviously, the ABA was not that good when it first started in 1967. Its most heralded star was Connie Hawkins—The Hawk—who was wrongly blackballed by the NBA because of an alleged dealing with a college basketball gambler. It is said that Connie was Julius Erving and Michael Jordan before they were Julius Erving and Michael Jordan. If that sounds like double talk, then consider this, there are those who say that Connie Hawkins was the best to ever play the game.

I played a little against him during my first year with the Warriors, but by then his game had declined. I believe that had he brought his youthful skills to the NBA and honed them further against the best of the best instead of the best of the rest in the early years of the ABA, he could have made a greater mark in NBA history. Connie, for sure, was a founding father of aerial artistry.

The Hawk was the ABA's first Most Valuable Player. He won the MVP during the 1967–1968 season with the Pittsburgh Pipers, which was the league's first championship team. He averaged 28.2 points a game with 12.6 rebounds a game, and he shot close to 80 percent from the free-throw line.

By the mid-1970s the ABA was coming on strong. The actual difference between the leagues was the age of the players. The ABA had mostly young players, while the NBA had mostly established players. One of the ABA stars who typified their youth and talent was Moses Malone. He was the first big name to make the successful leap from high school to the pros from St. Petersburg High School in Virginia to the Utah Stars. The Stars folded in 1975 and he played a year for the St. Louis Spirits. That team dissolved with the merger and Moses then came into the NBA to play with Houston and later Philadelphia. Although the Sixers had worked their way into a couple of NBA championship series behind McGinnis and Dr. J from the ABA, they didn't actually win one until Moses got there. When Moses retired from the NBA, he was the last player from the ABA.

The ABA had some great players who the NBA could no longer deny their own fans the opportunity of seeing, like Julius Erving, George McGinnis, Doug Moe, Mel Daniels, Dan Issel, George Gervin, David Thompson, Maurice Lucas and Roger Brown.

The ABA had a lot of talent, but they also had different rules that made the talent standout more. For instance, it was a less physical league and guys could maneuver around the basket without fear of losing any teeth or a portion of their vision.

There was a 30 seconds shot clock as compared to 24 seconds in the NBA. After the sixth foul, the player could remain in the game, but fouls beyond his sixth foul would give the opposing team two free throws and possession. But it was certainly worth it if you could keep guys like Connie Hawkins and Dr. J in the game! The Hawk from Brooklyn and Dr. J from Roosevelt (Long Island, New York) had moves and hang time that simply were not human.

When I played against The Doctor, I found him to be electrifying and efficient with everything he did. He was usually cool, calm and collected, but whenever he got intense he could take over a basketball game. Pure and simple! You weren't going to catch him, you weren't going to stop him, you weren't going to out-rebound him and chances were that you weren't going to get to the hole against him.

He was so graceful making moves to the basket that Dr. J should have gotten points just for the moves. He was so graceful that he looked like he was doing a ballet while flying toward the basket to stuff a basketball into a high cylinder. And that was an *effortless* move!

If he so desired, he could reverse or do some fan-arousing contortion while in the air. He could twist and change direction in midair while making up his mind to stuff the ball or lay it in with a finer role. When he was real intense on defense, he could sweep the board with a one-arm rebound. And, he could either make a great outlet pass or simply bring the ball down court and take it straight to the cup—coast to coast.

He had led his New Jersey Nets team to two ABA championships. He added another when he joined the Philadelphia 76ers in the NBA. When you told someone the Doctor was going to make a house call tonight, they knew what that meant—the Sixers were in town with one of the best-ever aerial artists, one of the most finesse athletes of any sport ever, one of the most dominating athletes of any sport ever, and still considered by a great many people as the best player ever.

Like Connie had been, Dr. J was the ABA'S Most Valuable Player. Three times!

When he later joined the NBA, leading the Sixers to four championship series and an NBA title, as well as winning the 1981 NBA MVP Award, Julius became, perhaps, the game's most dignified ambassador and remains so today, in my opinion.

One of his ABA MVP Awards was one shared in 1975 with George McGinnis. McGinnis had dominated at the power-forward spot in the ABA, like Karl Malone in the NBA during the 1990s. He was the ABA's most physical player and with the Hawk and The Doctor, all three are legends of their craft in ABA folklore.

The New York Knicks kept trying to get McGinnis, but playing with the Indiana Pacers in his hometown where he grew up and where he played college ball, McGinnis was having tremendous success and it would have taken an act of Congress to move him. With the merger on the horizon, he finally tried to sign with New York but couldn't because Philadelphia had his rights.

He breathed new life into a sad Sixers team and led them
to a first round appearance in the play-offs in 1976. Dr.
J joined the Sixers team a year later and the two of them
got busy and restored Philadelphia to basketball royalty.

They rolled through the play-offs en route to the
1977 NBA finals, where they met up with the Portland
Trailblazers and their brilliant coach Dr. Jack Ramsey.
Despite their great team, they lost to Portland. The
Trailblazers team featured a premier center in Bill
Walton and the late Maurice Lucas, the one forward in
the NBA who could matchup fairly with McGinnis, and
the cunning Bobby Gross at the other forward position.
Portland also had the two quickest guards in Johnny
Davis and Lionel Hollins. Dave Twardzick was their
sixth man. They basically ran right through the Lakers
and bounced them out of the playoffs. The extraordinary
quickness of Davis, Hollins forced the Lakers to go out
and get quick guards in the following years, namely
Norm Nixon and Michael Cooper.

The coolest guy in the ABA was George Gervin of
the San Antonio Spurs. The Iceman. When the merger
happened, it meant *The Iceman Cometh*!

In 1978, two years after the merger, he and David
"Skywalker" Thompson (who played with the Denver
Nuggets) were locked in a heavyweight dual—what was to
become the most memorable NBA scoring-title shoot-out.

The two were in a dead heat for the scoring title on
the final day of the season. David scored seventy-three
points against the Detroit Pistons earlier in the day.
Only Wilt Chamberlain had ever scored more points in
a game. Seventy-three points, who was guarding him?

Gervin would have to score sixty-three points to wrestle the title away. Seventy-three points was enough to put the Iceman on ice—right? Wrong. Gervin got sixty-three against the New Orleans Jazz. And who was guarding him? He beat David by .07 points with a scoring average of 27.22 points a game to David's 27.15.

David was a player in the mold of Dr. J, Michael Jordan and Kobe Bryant, but at six-four, he was a tad shorter, which made his gravity-defying feats even more entertaining. He had a forty-four-inch vertical leap and was called The Skywalker. His legend extends to the proportions as that of Earl Manigault "The Goat" of New York, as it is said both could snag money from the top of the backboard and leave change.

As was I, David grew up in the Baptist church. His father was a well-regarded deacon. But whereas I grew up in a small family in a beach city on the West Coast, David grew up with a large family in a rural area in a small town near Charlotte.

He had attended North Carolina State University, where he dismantled the UCLA string of NCAA championships, leading the Wolfpack to the 1974 NCAA championship. At age twenty-three, he became the highest-paid player in the history of team sports. When Denver joined the NBA in the merger year, it was David who led the Nuggets to a Western Division title in their very first year. And it was The Skywalker who finished first in NBA All-Star voting that year.

KAREEM ABDUL-JABBAR

XV

HOOKING UP WITH THE BIG FELLA

He courageously aligned himself with black athletes threatening to boycott the 1968 Olympics and supported the fisted, black-unity demonstration of Tommy Smith and John Carlos after they won the hundred-meter gold and bronze medals, respectively, in the 1968 games in Mexico City. Kareem also had been a central figure among the premiere African American sports personalities who stood firmly behind Muhammad Ali when the world heavyweight champion clung to his principles concerning the Vietnam War.

For quite a long time, I had visions of success playing with the Lakers under Coach Jerry West and alongside Kareem Abdul-Jabbar. What player from Southern California wouldn't have wanted that opportunity? I signed with the Los Angeles Lakers in 1977.

Jerry West was the guard version of Rick Barry. He was every bit the same perfectionist, every bit the same competitive level, and every bit the same complete player.

Kareem had become, by far, the most dominant player in all of basketball. He had only won one title to that point, but titles in the NBA are won by teams and are hard to come by. As an individual player, Kareem stood alone at a higher level.

There will forever be disagreement about who was the greatest center in NBA history. For those who use championships as a barometer, Bill Russell is the man. For those who want to talk about mano a mano in the lane, then the most dominant force was the late Wilt Chamberlain. Then there are those who say that if Bill Walton had had the good fortune to have a healthier career, he would have set a new plateau. And, of course, there's "Shaq Daddy" (Shaquille O'Neal), who had many of the talents of all the above.

But if you want athleticism, excellence, intelligence, dominance, and completeness in every facet of the game, then Kareem is the guy. He was far more versatile than all the others. He could give you the defense and intelligence of Russell and the offense and dominant presence of Chamberlain, he was far more athletic than Walton was, and he was far more agile than Shaq. He could do everything each of them could and more. Maybe on a given night, Walton could outplay him—or even Moses Malone, Bob Lanier, or Artis Gilmore. Heck, even my Warriors teammate Clifford Ray could give him all he could handle on nights when Clifford was in beast mode. But for consistency day in and day out and top performance in every facet of the game, that's Kareem.

Every player at the pro level had performed well at the high-school and college levels (at least those who went to college). But Kareem dominated at every level along the way with his unique athleticism.

Although the late Walt Hazzard (Abdul Rahman) and Gail Goodrich teams got the UCLA championship wagon rolling, it was the Lew Alcindor/Kareem Abdul-Jabbar teams that established the dynasty. He guided the Bruins to a three-year record of 88–2, and one loss is attributable to a badly scratched eye he suffered just before meeting the second-ranked Houston Cougars led by Elvin Hayes.

He was the first player to be named the NCAA tournament's Most Outstanding Player three times. He completely ruled the college level—so much so that the NCAA outlawed the dunk while he was at UCLA.

He was the first player chosen in the 1969 draft, selected by the Milwaukee Bucks. He became Rookie of the Year, averaging 28.8 points and fourteen rebounds a game in that first year. In his second year, he and Oscar Robertson led Milwaukee to an NBA title.

After earning NBA MVP honors in 1971, 1972, and 1974, he moved on to the Los Angeles Lakers prior to the 1975–1976 season, two years before me. We both were UCLA alums, and we both had converted to Islam. However, we were not as close as many people thought based on all that we had in common. We were friends, but not in the sense of confidants and running buddies.

I looked up to Kareem as a truly great basketball player and as an intelligent and spiritual person. It is common knowledge that he is highly intelligent. But he is a serious thinker, and is global in his perspectives.

In my opinion, as good a basketball player as he was and as smart as he is, he easily could have been self-serving and egotistical. But Kareem was the exact opposite; he was a deep humanitarian. He was observant and concerned about things going on around him—his immediate environment, our country, and the world.

He grew up in New York City and matriculated at UCLA during the height of the Pan-African Black Consciousness Movement.

He courageously aligned himself with black athletes threatening to boycott the 1968 Olympics and supported the fisted, black-unity demonstration of Tommy Smith and John Carlos after they won the hundred-meter gold and bronze medals, respectively, in the 1968 games in Mexico City. Kareem also had been a central figure among the premiere African American sports personalities who stood firmly behind Muhammad Ali when the world heavyweight champion clung to his principles concerning the Vietnam War.

He always had a particularly keen Pan-African perspective. I was amazed at how keenly aware he was of the causes and effects of political and social issues affecting people all around the world.

However, he only shared his thoughts with those of whom he was certain could relate to what he had to impart. To know Kareem well enough to have real conversation with him is a privilege. I was familiar with a lot of social issues; he would take it deeper and, at the same time, be even more simplistic and realistic.

The media considered him as being standoffish to them. In reality, they simply couldn't relate to him. Reporters only wanted a sound bite or quote to meet deadlines and satisfy their editors. They generally asked the same kind of questions day in and day out, about a game that they just saw.

To what do you attribute tonight's win? What was the key to tonight's game? What did you think when the opponent seemed to be making a comeback? What do you think about the coach's decision in the last minute? Those were the kind of questions we had to answer repeatedly. Same questions, night after night. We understood the media brought the hype to the game, but freshening up the questions from time to time would not have hurt.

Most athletes weren't approached nearly as much as Kareem, so most didn't mind speaking with the media. Sports reporters didn't seem to understand why some guys didn't mind doing interviews and why some were uninterested. Their interpretation seemed to be that, if you didn't sing and dance when they asked a question, you were an enigmatic character. This also was at a point in time when African American reporters were a rare sight at the press tables or in the locker rooms, and most of them were from African American newspapers or radio stations. The breaking of that racial barrier was in progress during these years.

A sports reporter getting a quote from Kareem was like a city-hall reporter getting a quote from the mayor. More so than even the coach, his quotes could give substance to the story. Whether he understood it or not, he actually could have controlled the media.

Kareem, as an intelligent, realistic man, understood
that basketball was an important part of his life but not
more important than life itself. He understood that early
on as a collegian. There were more important things going
on in the world than the fact that he may have had thirty
points, eighteen rebounds, four blocked shots and taken
control of a game at a crucial moment. That was his job.
My perception from talking a lot with Kareem was that he
was an advocate for a better tomorrow for all mankind.

Kareem knew that, like him, I had been an all-American
in college; I had won Rookie of the Year honors; I had an
NBA championship under my belt and knew what it would
take to get another; and I was considered an unselfish player.

What was real cool and perhaps more important, I
had an outside shot and, by then, was an established
NBA forward who could help open up the inside game.
The game's most dominant center and a solid forward
coming together is a good scenario, no matter who they
are or from where they came. That we were UCLA alumni
and Islam converts only complemented the scenario.
They were not essential issues and did not play a major
role in our personal relationship.

In addition to hooking up with the greatest player in the
game, I would also be reunited with my old Santa Barbara
High School teammate Don Ford. Plus, I would be returning
to the area where I had played college ball and be closer
to my family. I was so enthusiastic, I might have taken a
drastic pay cut to be a Laker. But the contract experience
with the Warriors made it clear that this was a business.

Signing with the Lakers as a free agent caused quite
a stir with regard to compensation. The issue of free

agency in professional sports was evolving during this period of time.

During my negotiations with the Lakers, the NBA was in the process of adopting a ruling that if a team signs a free agent from another team, then the signing team must appropriately compensate the free agent's former team. It's a frequent occurrence now, but it was something new in 1977.

By now, I was considered a premiere player in the NBA—a very premiere player with my best years ahead of me. As far as the Warriors were concerned, the only player the Lakers had who could compensate their loss of my services was Kareem. It was an obvious, overstated, and transparent negotiations ploy. Kareem definitely wasn't going anywhere, even if it meant that I would not be going to the Lakers. And I was definitely not going to be with the Warriors, even if I wasn't going to be with the Lakers. But again, free agency was a new element, and what would transpire would serve as a benchmark for years and deals to follow.

The end result was that the Lakers would have to compensate the Warriors with $250,000 and a first-round draft choice the following year.

There was a lot of criticism in the bay Area about my leaving the Warriors. Loyal fans were frustrated. Fans had not yet become accustomed to cornerstone-type players up and leaving. They don't necessarily blame the player; for them, it's just not the way things are supposed to be. As steadfast as I was about my position with the Warriors owners reneging on their promise, on the other side of the ledger, I was queasy about leaving a lot of good people in the organization, as well as fans and friends in the Bay Area.

There were some undue criticism and untrue rumors as to why I was severing ties with Golden State. The undue and untrue criticism ranged from rumors of personal conflicts with Rick Barry and Phil Smith to total team dissention. There was absolutely no truth to any of that.

I had the desire to leave for two years, and it was time to move on. I honored my contract. Since I pretty much had kept things to myself concerning my disenchantment with the Warriors management and their failing to keep their promise, no one really knew anything. It is not my nature to cry foul, particularly since I had no one nor anything to back me up. So engaging a media campaign about the genesis of the departure was not anything that even crossed my mind. I took it all in stride, did my job when in the Warriors' uniform, and took action on my terms when it was time. Those involved knew what the truths were, and that's all that really mattered.

The Warriors did put an offer on the table some time during mid-spring of 1977. They were considering Phil and myself to be the nucleus of the future. It was an interesting offer, but I knew it was in my best interest to leave. Frankly, I didn't just tear up the offer. I kept the dialogue open but never heard anything compelling. The dialogue never healed the wound I felt as a slight. As an unintended consequence, I was able to use the offer as a base to help strengthen my negotiating posture with the Lakers.

With my popularity in Southern California, there was a groundswell of fan support for the Lakers to acquire me. Once it was clear that Laker management was truly interested, I knew I was going there. All they had to do was come close to the Warriors' offer.

Although the Warriors' offer was handsome, remaining was not a consideration. I actually and truthfully had been preparing for life without basketball if it had come to that. I looked into law school and postgraduate programs. I did not spend lavishly. Fortunately, the Lakers wanted me there as much as I wanted to be there, and their offer turned out to be even better than the Warriors, and the compensation issue was worked out.

In addition to going back and forth between Golden State and the Los Angeles Laker negotiations, I was experiencing some off-court stress from another dimension.

I met and dated a really nice young lady named Joy, and after my first season with the Golden State Warriors, we were married. During my third and final season with the Warriors, we experienced the loss of a baby daughter who died a few months after birth due to a heart defect. It was a traumatic experience for Joy and me. At one point, it appeared death was inevitable, and we were in a horrible state of confusion of whether to bring the child home or leave her in the hospital, away from home. It was very difficult, and there was no right answer, because what we wanted was for the child to live.

Also, during much of the short-term marriage, I was the target of a paternity suit from an outside party I had a brief encounter with prior to meeting Joy. Thus, there was little opportunity to enjoy being married, and finally the marriage went sour and ended in divorce.

It had a very bad effect on me. I came from a strong family with model parents who had been together for some thirty-plus years. Of all the things I had to deal with, this was the one thing for which I didn't have a solution. A major aspect of life had gone wrong, and I couldn't fix it. In retrospect, the marriage hadn't worked largely due to my own immaturity. Both of us were naïve about a lot of things—at least I was. The paternity suit was a situation that we construed as threatening. As a couple, we became unglued as to its implications, but in reality, we had no reason to be frightened. We simply needed to pull together and deal with it.

We also spun out in different directions in the aftermath of the death of the child and, again, missed an opportunity to become closer. But that's what happens in some marriages, particularly when you're young. You can easily lose composure when the going gets tough, and at a time when composure is what you need most. It takes a lot to keep a marriage happy and healthy. The commitment was there, but like so many other things in my life, I thought it would be easy.

In just a three-year time span, at the ripe old age of twenty-four, I experienced a bad business deal, the death of a child, a paternity suit, and a failed marriage.

Signing with the Lakers and having the opportunity to move on down the road made me whole again. It was truly a phoenix rising in my soul. Life again was beautiful.

JAMAAL WILKES

First Year Laker

XVI
FIRST YEAR LAKER

One aspect of my game that was greatly enhanced by Norm Nixon's presence was getting out on the wing to match his speed. He ran the fast break beyond textbook perfection. He could see the court extremely well. He was heady and could pass exceptionally well. He could stop on a dime and make that picturesque rise and fall-away jumper that got nothing but net. And believe me when I tell you, Norm always made the right decision with the ball. Playing with Kareem was a dream come true; playing with Norm was exciting.

The owner of the Los Angeles Lakers was Jack Kent Cooke. At the time of my arrival, he was going through a divorce, and his settlement made the *Guinness Book of World Records* as the most expensive. He was exiled in Las Vegas. It was in Las Vegas where my representatives and I met with him to finalize the deal.

Bill Sharman was president and general manager. Jerry West was in his second year as head coach for the Los Angeles Lakers. He had an innovative system of using a defensive coordinator and an offensive coordinator, like football programs. Jack McCloskey was the defensive coordinator. Stan Albeck was the offensive coordinator.

The man actually running the Lakers organization was Chick Hearn. Like most Southern Californians, I grew up listening to Chick Hearn on radio broadcasts of Laker home and away games. The way he could call a game with his picturesque radio broadcasting was almost better than being at the game itself. Hearing him go on and on about Jerry West, Elgin Baylor, Tommy Hawkins, and other Laker players was every young boy's fantasy. He'd vividly used the radio dial as the court and say things like, "West is bringing the ball up court, left to right on your dial." Or broadcasting a midcourt offense, he'd say, "Here's West, yo-yoing [the basketball] up-down and signaling the offensive play." Everybody's favorite, of course, was when Wilt or, later, Kareem Abdul-Jabbar would score, and Chick would say, "Here's the ball into Wilt; he turns, SLAM DUNK!"

Years later, as a Laker, I would affectionately call him "Golden Throat," and he would immortalize my jump shot as the "twenty-foot layup."

I took tremendous pride in my twenty-foot layup, and I must share credit with Bill Sharman. Bill had a

Hall of Fame career with the Boston Celtics and had a great coaching career, including the Lakers. He was eventually also inducted into the Naismith Hall of Fame as a coach. I knew about his career as a coach with the Utah Stars in the ABA and in the NBA. He was well respected among players, not only as a coach but also as an innovator, motivator, and a class act in general. He's the one who started the morning shoot around and got Wilt Chamberlain to buy into it when no one thought Wilt would ever do it.

He captured a championship when he coached that great 1971–1972 Laker team led by Jerry West, Gail Goodrich, and Wilt Chamberlain and that won thirty-three games in a row. The team also featured another future coach of mine, Pat Riley. Other key players and major contributors to that history-making team were Happy Hairston, Jim McMillan, Keith Erickson, Flynn Robinson, John Trapp and rookie Jim Cleamons.

Typically, early in my career, I would hit the proverbial wall and go into a shooting slump usually around early February. When I went into one of these shooting slumps, I would work harder on defense and rebounding to give the coach a reason to keep me in the game.

One day during one these slumps in 1980, Bill Sharman called me over to sit in the bleachers after practice to visit. I was petrified and thought he was going to tell me I had been traded. I had the utmost respect for Bill but rarely came into contact with him as president of the team.

He had a pen and paper in his hand and asked me to sit with him in the bleachers. He drew two circles and the words direction and distance on the paper. One circle he drew nine inches across it, and the other he drew eighteen inches across it. He said the nine-inch circle was the ball, the eighteen-inch circle was the rim, and that I had nine inches, or *all this room*, for error. He said as long as I had the right direction on my shot, I could easily adjust the distance, and if I didn't have the right direction, then it may be something mechanical with the shot. If it was something mechanical, then I'd have to review the basics of my shot. Having Bill explain this to me in his gentle manner crystallized it in my mind, boosted my confidence, and I was *so* pumped.

Thereafter, I never had a shooting slump for more than a couple games in a row, and that was the birth of my jump shot becoming as sure as a layup—a twenty-foot layup.

When the Lakers camp opened that year at the University of San Diego, I was feeling quite rejuvenated and looking forward to an interesting new life and playing with the best player in basketball, Kareem Abdul-Jabbar.

On the Lakers that year were Lou Hudson, Earl Tatum, Don Chaney, Tom Abernathy, James Edwards, Kermit Washington, Kareem, and my former teammate from Santa Barbara High School, Don Ford. Adrian Dantley and Ernie DiGregerio later joined the team.

The Lakers had three first-draft picks: Kenny Carr out of North Carolina State, Brad Davis out of Maryland, and Norm Nixon from Duquesne University in Pittsburgh, Pennsylvania.

During the previous year's play-off run, the Lakers had been beaten badly at the guard position by the Portland

Trailblazers, which featured the blazing tandem of Lionel Hollins and Johnny Davis. Of course Portland also had Bill Walton, who kicked the outlet pass better than anyone who's ever played the game, and Maurice Lucas.

Johnny Davis was the quickest player I've ever played against. He may have been the fastest ever in terms of pure quickness. I played against him in college and in the NBA's Pacific Division and clearly understood what the Lakers had been up against when they faced him. The only guy I ever played against who could match his quickness was Spud Webb of the Atlanta Hawks and Nate "Tiny" Archibald with the Kansas City Kings.

The Lakers had wanted to shore up the guard position with more speed. "Sweet Lou" Hudson and Don Chaney were experienced and solid veterans but were in the twilight of their careers. Lou was an excellent floor leader and shooter, and Don was a defensive specialist noted for his long reach and defensive savvy. The Lakers also added Ron "Iron Man" Boone who was one of the top all-around guards during his 13 years in the ABA and NBA.

Hollins and Davis made a clear statement that it was going to be a new day in the NBA, and it was going to be about speed. If you were going to match up with the Portland Trailblazers, you'd better bring some speed.

The only guy we had to actually match up with them was Norm Nixon. Brad Davis, who came into the league after his junior year at Maryland, had the potential to upgrade the Lakers' speed, though he was not in the speed class of Nixon, Davis, and Hollins.

There was a hitch in the team's efforts to acquire guards with more speed. The hitch stemmed from an apparent miscommunication between Coach West and General Manager Bill Sharman with regard to the acquisition of DiGregerio.

Ernie was an exceptional ball handler, a good scorer, and an overall exciting ball player. But he had a conspicuous absence of defensive skills. That could not possibly sit well with Jerry West, a Hall of Fame perfectionist at both ends of the court and one of the all-time great defenders.

It was widely reported that Jerry was concerned with the DiGregerio acquisition because it hampered his ability to utilize Brad. Ernie and Brad had similar games. But Brad was younger, quicker, taller, and had defensive skills. He had talent and was equipped to become a good defensive NBA player for years to come. Brad went on to have a fine career with the Dallas Mavericks. Ernie D., on the other hand, was an exciting offensive player but was not as strong defensively as our other guards.

As it turned out, the whole issue became a moot point because, luckily, Norm emerged as the club's point guard and eventually went on to become one of the premiere point guards in the league.

My first game as a Laker was one of the strangest.

We opened up in Milwaukee against the Bucks. Milwaukee's first-round draft selection was Kent Benson, a six-eleven center who was one of the stars on Indiana's 1977 NCAA championship team. They were looking for him to be the franchise player that Kareem had been for the Bucks.

Benson weighed in at about 240 pounds and had a strong physical inside game. The game was only seconds old when he elbowed Kareem viciously in the midsection, knocking the wind out of Kareem. Kareem doubled over in obvious distress.

This was during Kareem's earlier years, a period when he was dominating every which way with his finesse and total-package game. There was no way for anyone to possibly stop Kareem. His finesse was as devastating as the power of Shaquille O'Neal. Double- and triple-teams couldn't contain Kareem.

What many teams tried to do was play two or three of their more physical guys who would be willing to go beyond the rules on Kareem (*remember, I also played against him*). They would do this by wearing him down, laying into him to impede his effectiveness. They leaned and pushed or did whatever it took. *Whatever* it took.

When I was with the Warriors, Clifford Ray's only chance was to be in ultimate beast mode and still get some help. Keeping Kareem under forty points was a good night. You couldn't allow him any kind of room to shoot his patented skyhook. If you had fifteen fouls to give, you used all fifteen. He wasn't Elgin Baylor, Connie Hawkins, Michael Jordan, or Julius Erving, but he could get to the bucket or get a shot off a million different ways if there was any kind of seam.

From an opponent's standpoint, if you didn't play beyond the rules, Kareem would beat you single-handedly with an array of left and right-handed dunks, soft bank shots, and that unstoppable, patented skyhook. I know full well, because Clifford, George Johnson, and myself would have to deal with him. Principally it was Clifford and George, but I would come over to help in the double- or triple-team. Forget about it! Even with triple-teaming tactics, the Big Fellow was good enough for thirty-five points a night.

Meanwhile, Kareem's no dummy.

He knew what was going on—that they were playing him tough and beyond the rules. Very little of what they did was overt. It most often was out of view of the referees, who, in my opinion, should have been more attentive to this particular game within the game. I would never say they let it happen, but they could have done much more. When Kareem registered his concern to the referee, he didn't get any justice. In their defense, the refs tried to keep their eyes on things at times but felt they had nine other guys to watch as well as control the benches and keep tab of the clock. Still, given the prevalence of this outside-the-lines gamesmanship, the refs could have done better.

Thus, when Kareem stepped out onto the court, it was war—pure and simple.

It was him against the world for forty-eight, rugged, UFC-style minutes. Suckering Kareem with a cheap-shot elbow in the solar plexus to start a new season was something you would only do if you had a death wish or were looking for your family to collect on an insurance policy.

After the Kent Benson shiver blow, the next few moments were bizarre. I didn't exactly see what happened, but I heard it.

As I was coming off a baseline screen and darting toward the sideline to receive a pass, I heard a loud CRACK!

I looked around and saw Kent Benson stretched out on the floor. He was out cold!

Then I looked up and away from Benson, and there was a wild-eyed Kareem going through some funky kung-fu moves in preparation to deal with any on-comers. Keep in mind, Kareem is a martial-arts expert who was trained by Bruce Lee, who was his very good friend. Kareem was bouncing lightly on his toes in an intense warrior-like trance.

Everybody was shocked. First of all, we were shocked to see Benson with his lights out. Cold. Secondly, we were surprised that the basketball court had become a battlefield.

A few of us, I don't know if we were brave or stupid, approached Kareem. He gradually calmed down.

Kareem was ejected from the game and, worse, suffered a severely fractured hand from his knockout blow. He was gone for a nice chunk of the new season. Talk about man's best plans. There I was, realizing a dream come true and taking the floor for the start of the season with Kareem Abdul-Jabbar. We didn't even get a good sweat going, and he was gone.

A few months later came the Kermit Washington blast that almost ended the life of Houston Rocket Rudy Tomjanovich.

In that incident, Kermit somehow got involved with a near scuffle at midcourt. Several players moved to the area to calm the situation.

Rudy approached Kermit from the blindside to help calm things down. But it was in such an awkward angle

and manner that Kermit could not possibly distin-
guish him from an ally or attacker, or even exactly
who it was coming toward him. Just knowing it was
Rudy approaching him would have been enough to put
him at ease, because Rudy is a voice-of-reason type
of guy who everybody liked and respected. Even if he
were the last guy on the court in an all-out war, no one
would want to get violent with someone as likeable as
Rudy.

But Kermit had no way of knowing who it was.

Kermit let him have it, a haymaker that crushed the
side of Rudy's face and had him laid up in a hospital for
an extensive period of time. It ended his career.

Once again, shock on the basketball court. This
time it was a lot more dramatic because it was Rudy
Tomjanovich, a highly respected and well-liked NBA pro
on the floor. No one knew how extensive the injury was,
but whatever the injury and reason for him being on the
floor, and whoever it was involved, that was the wrong
guy to be punched out.

That was Rudy T. on the floor! Something had gone
dreadfully wrong.

By the time things were sorted out, every single soul
on the court felt remorse, whether they were involved
or not. We knew our basketball fraternity would get a
public-relations black eye.

One of the greatest guys to know and easiest to get
along with, Rudy T., had become a completely innocent
victim of a major assault—on an NBA basketball court
in front of a packed house in a televised game. We knew
that the public perception would be that if something like

this could happen to Tomjanovich, clearly we, as players, were out of control.

And almost as bad, the assailant was Kermit Washington, who also was a great guy to know and respect. He was an intelligent, powerfully built athlete at about six-nine who had averaged twenty points and rebounds a game in his senior year at American Continental International University. Only Elgin Baylor, the University of Seattle legend and Laker great, could make that claim.

Kermit was at the disposal of the National Basketball Association administration to be used as a billboard to end fighting. He was unjustly slapped with a tremendous fine and suspension. Everybody knew it was unjust, but everybody knew it was a billboard message. We also knew it had to be done, thus, no one could really say anything too loudly. None of us, including Kermit, are saints, but he was one of the last guys who you would have expected to be in that predicament.

Kermit was a great rebounder and low-post player. He did have a reputation as a physical player but not a menacing character. All of a sudden, with one incident that, as bad as it was, was a freaky misfortune, and he became a villain. His image was blemished, and he was subsequently traded to Boston.

I understood why the NBA acted so drastically, but I also thought it was greatly unreasonable. His haymaker was purely in self-defense, for starters. It was awful and should never have happened, but it did, even though Kermit was only protecting himself. On the other side of the ledger, anything less than a drastic disciplinary

action following such a horrific incident would not have
sent an adequate antiviolence message.

As if the incidents with Kareem and Kermit weren't
enough of a damper on the year, I later suffered a hairline
fracture on the pinky finger of my left hand while diving
for a loose ball.

The darn thing just would not heal according to the
book or anyone's expectations.

Not only did I miss more games than what was normal
for that kind of injury, but when I did get back onto the
court, it was easily aggravated and hurt my game.

The euphoric feeling I'd had when I signed was
dampened. I felt we had a great team, and this was exactly
the situation I wanted to be in, but the dog ate the script.
Right out of the box, we lost our top gun. Then we lost
our power forward and key rebounder. And the newly
acquired superstar free agent was nursing a nagging
injury. I was not performing like the Jamaal Wilkes
the Lakers had hired. You know these things happen in
sports, but in your mind, you see the window of opportunity becoming foggy.

We did have some bright spots. Norm Nixon and
Adrian Dantley were coming on like gangbusters.
Particularly Norm! He had come on real strong, far
surpassing expectations. He was about as fast as
Portland's Johnny Davis, who I've said is one of the
quickest I've ever played against.

Norm was scoring in double figures. He was among
the league leaders in assists and steals, and he was an
outstanding defensive player.

At Duquesne University, Norm had been an even bigger scorer. He averaged more than twenty points a game in his junior and senior years. Thus, he could have been a big offensive weapon had the coaches chosen to go to him to score more. But he was such a terrific ball handler and scoring threat that he would draw defenses away from other guys and create opportunities for Kareem and open shots for the perimeter players. With Norm being able to penetrate so well and with Kareem in the middle, you don't want to get too cute. Defenses had to play us honestly, except when Kareem was hot and forced them to double- and triple-team him. So Norm's job was to keep it simple and run the offense off of Kareem. When necessary, Norm would break his man down and blast to the bucket for two. He could break down any defender at any point in time at will. He always finished among the top scorers.

Playing with Kareem was a big change for me as well. The Warriors had been a forward-oriented team. In fact, had I stayed as the heir apparent to Rick Barry's role with the team, we would have been a forward-oriented team for a long time.

But with the Lakers and a youthful Kareem, we were a center-oriented team. Plus we had Adrian Dantley, who had one of the strongest inside games of anybody in the league. Using the boxing analogy of pound for pound and inch for inch, Adrian was the best inside player. When you consider his size, listed generously at six-five, he was nothing less than phenomenal in the things he was able to do under the basket. Plus we had two more big men with strong inside games in Kermit and Kenny

Carr. The Lakers had put together a really good and very balanced squad, and playing under Jerry West, it was of playoff caliber.

As the starting forward opposite Adrian, I still was considered the power forward. Defensively, I always had the assignment of guarding the power forward on opposing teams, although on offense, Adrian had a more power-forward type of game. He was awesome on the offensive boards. With his low-post moves and powerful body, he would often put on an offensive rebounding clinic.

We were a very good interior team. There was always a traffic jam in the middle. To give the team an added dimension and complement our inside-scoring threat, I worked on making my contributions from the perimeter and learned to play without the ball. This is where I became even more appreciative of the tutelage of Rick and was able to put to use the offensive skills I had learned from him at Golden State.

Once I got my outside shot going, it made it a difficult decision for opponents thinking about double- and triple-teaming Kareem. I became the second scoring option. In addition to having me on the outside moving to an open spot, Kareem also could easily dish off to Adrian under-neath or Norm cutting down the lane.

One of the entertaining and motivating aspects about the seasons was that Adrian and I had a personal competition to get down the court on fast-break opportunities to score. We knew that once we got into a half-court offense, we were unlikely to get the rock because it was going inside to Kareem, and rightfully so for textbook basketball— get the ball to the big fella.

Adrian and I joked, and I laughed about it. We would say that the only way to get some points was to haul ass down court before the half-court game clicked in. Plus, Adrian was an ex-Notre Dame guy who had been a freshman on the team that ended the UCLA eighty-eight-game winning streak. We had the makings for what became a hilarious and friendly competition. More importantly, we didn't talk a lot of stuff; we just played hard for one-upmanship and the last laugh. Plus, we had Norm pushing the rock, and that made it even more fun.

One aspect of my game that was greatly enhanced was getting out on the wing to match the speed of Norm. He could see the court extremely well. He was heady and could pass exceptionally well. He could stop on a dime and make that picturesque rise and fall-away jumper that got nothing but net. And believe me when I tell you, Norm made good decisions with the ball. Playing with Kareem was a dream-come-true; playing with Norm was exciting. But as a whole, our season was not great, even though we obviously had the horses and a great knowledgeable coach in Jerry West.

My finger problem never went away. I was in and out of the lineup. It's very difficult for the team to get its act together when a starter is inconsistent. And then when I was playing, things weren't going well for me because of the discomfort of the darn thing. I was in a catch-22. I didn't want to let the team down by being AWOL, but when I got on the court, I wasn't effective catching the ball, handling it, shooting it or rebounding. I was in a twilight zone, and during a time when we should have been getting stronger as a team, we weren't improving because I couldn't bring my A game to the table.

We did make it to the play-offs, but the Seattle Supersonics knocked us out in the first round. It was a low point by Lakers standards, but it set the table for a new era of Los Angeles Lakers basketball.

We later found out my injury was much worse and more complicated than it had been assumed. As it turned out, a fragment of the fractured bone in my finger had gone through the center of a preexisting cyst. A hand specialist, Dr. Herb Stark, made the discovery.

I had off-season surgery to correct the real problem and bounced back with a productive season the following year.

During my first two seasons with the Lakers, I was still playing power forward. But guys like Maurice Lucas, George McGinnis, and Lonnie Shelton were redefining the position.

When we went up against Seattle in the 1978 and 1979 play-offs with me at power forward, it was difficult hanging in there with Jack Sikma and Lonnie Shelton. Sikma would just about knock my teeth down my throat every time he went up with a jumper on me. It wasn't just me. It was his style of play. When he would shoot his jumper, he would flip out his elbows and clip the defender on the chops. It frankly was an excellent offensive technique of his to create space. Shelton was just a beefy bruiser who played without regard to the fact that I (or, for that matter, anyone else) was of the human species. He was too strong for me. He was too strong for most other guys as well, pure and simple.

We had a group of inside players, but the game was changing before our very eyes.

If we were going to get past Seattle and advance deeper into the play-offs, we had to match up with their power.

Off the court during my early years with the Lakers, I met a genuine dazzling beauty queen from Montego Bay, Jamaica, my wife Valerie.

Jamaal and Valerie Wilkes

XVII

THE MONTEGO BAY INVASION

She looked like a mesmerizing supermodel that just stepped off of a colorful poster advertising Jamaican vacations. She had an infectious effervescence that carbonated my own spirits.

At the time we met, Valerie was a flight attendant with Trans World Airlines. She had been in Los Angeles visiting some friends from Jamaica. Her friends, Gil and Carol, were also acquaintances with my former UCLA teammate Tommy Curtis. Unbeknown to her and me, we became the principal characters of a matchmaking scheme.

Her Jamaican friends got Tommy to bring her by my place after a game with Cleveland. During this period of time, I was very apprehensive about anything that resembled a serious relationship. The divorce and paternity issue were behind me, but my approach with lady friends was immature, if not hardened.

At this point in time, I was more concerned about working myself into the favor of Laker fans. The power-forward position was being redefined by guys who were taller, beefier, stronger, and, frankly, bringing a mightier game to the table. I had made my mark in the NBA playing inside, so I could play the position at the highest level, but night after night, for thirty-five to forty minutes up and down the court at warp speed, grinding it out in the paint with these new behemoths didn't bode well for having a long career for someone my size. Fortunately, with Kareem and Adrian, my game was becoming strictly finesse.

When I first got into the league, I had decent size to compete well as a NBA forward, good fundamentals, and surprising finesse, and that worked. It worked basically because I had the advantage of playing what is now described as a small-forward game, and the beefier guys could not defend against me.

But that was changing before my eyes. From one perspective, one could say I was helping to define the role of the small forward.

Some of these new guys, like Lucas and Shelton, had both brute force and finesse going for them, and they could deal with me. Thus, it was always a battle, and in the play-offs, I was coming up short.

We had not gone deep into the play-offs, and we had to make adjustments. In that situation, you don't know what kind of career or personnel changes are in the wind.

So the first time I met Valerie, I did not know that Tommy was bringing her by when they came. When I first saw her, it was straight-up WOW! You could've stuck a fork in me, because I was done. All those issues, insecurities, apprehensions, and the rest of that *bull* went flying out the window. When God put this woman together, he outperformed himself. Now keep in mind, we are talking about Los Angeles, where eight out of every ten women have movie-star looks. On a scale of one to ten, this lady was a perfect *eleven*! Was I captivated? You bet. Try spellbound.

Valerie and I now have three wonderful adult children, and I still wake up each morning pinching myself because I'm living in a dream world with this beautiful woman, who is twice as beautiful on the inside and whose persona is angelic. I was way over my head then, and when I look at her now, I still think I'm way over my head.

She had a pure, charming personality that is unique to Jamaicans. She was so beautiful. She looked like a mesmerizing supermodel that just stepped off a poster advertising Jamaican vacations.

As it turned out, she was working a Los Angeles flight for four consecutive weeks. *Oh really*, I thought to myself upon hearing that news flash. Boy, oh boy! I was having an anxiety attack.

Could it be possible that she would make time for me?

She gave me the thumbs up and said it was possible. Man, when she said that, I thought I'd died and gone to heaven. It didn't matter what would happen after that. This West Indian goddess had consented to having a

date with an introverted gym rat who was trying to make
a living playing basketball and who, at present, wasn't
exactly taking the world by storm.

We were able to spend plenty of time together to get
to know each other. I got the *skinny* on her background.
She was a graduate of Brooklyn College. Her home was
Montego Bay, Jamaica, but she resided in New York. She
told me about her family in Jamaica. She told me about
the culture. I couldn't wait to visit the place that could
produce such a wonder.

The time we began spending together certainly
indicated that we were rounding second base. All of my
past issues seemed to have been in a different world—
another life long, long ago.

My life had just gotten better. She had an infectious
effervescence that carbonated my own spirits. My outlook
on everything in life began blossoming for the first time.
With everything else I had done up to that time, I had
been feeling my way, trying to make the grade and get to
the next point in life. Now the whole picture started to
come into focus.

That summer I visited her native home, Montego Bay.
The area and the country made quite an impression on me.

It was very British. It was very mellow. The people
were warm, and the beaches were as breathtaking as
they looked in the travel brochures.

Bob Marley was going strong. He was like a prophet
in Jamaica. I learned that another famous Jamaican,
Marcus Garvey of African American history fame, was a
national hero there. I was familiar with Marcus Garvey

and the Garvey Movement but was unaware of his esteemed stature in Jamaica. It was a spellbinding place. It was as captivating as Valerie.

One particular day, we were sitting in a car along the countryside and admiring the ocean and the wonderful Jamaica scenery. All of a sudden, out of nowhere, this older black man popped up. He was very dark skinned. He had a big round face with large features. He stood about six-four.

Now, there we were in the countryside with nothing but space all around, and presto, here's this guy standing in front of us.

"Is this woman your wife?" he asked.

"No," I said.

"Do you love this woman?" he asked.

I said, "Sort of."

I was really getting even more uncomfortable about this big dude who just dropped in from out of nowhere.

"'Sort of?' Is this your woman?" he asked.

I said, "Yeah. Yeah, you could say that."

"Well now, what kind of answer is that?" he responded. "Either you love her, or you don't."

I didn't know what business it was of his, but he was right.

Then he started preaching. He was fascinating and spellbinding.

He spoke for forty-five minutes about the virtues of a good woman. He spoke about the virtues of treating people right. The central theme of his message was that the problem of the world is that we don't tell people we love them. Today people are more inclined to tell their loved ones that they love them, but at that point in time, it wasn't a common occurrence.

When he concluded, he asked me for a favor.

I said, "Sure."

He asked me to give him a lift downtown.

Now, I was really wondering if I'd gone nuts. This guy appeared like magic, and now he wanted to bum a ride to town.

When we got downtown, he wanted to be dropped off at a tavern. Turned out, the tavern is just down the street from where Valerie's parents had spent their honeymoon. He invited me in for a drink. I said, "No thanks," but gave him a few bucks to have a drink on me.

I started to think it was some kind of setup. It was just too weird. Valerie said the guy apparently was just a country preacher.

I still was befuddled. I still couldn't understand where he had come from in the first place when he appeared so suddenly. No way did it make sense. (I even feel awkward telling the story.)

Valerie said he might have been an "Obie Man" or what is known in neighboring Haiti as a "Voodoo Man."

I just looked at her and decided to go with her country-preacher notion.

I also made up my mind about something else. I wanted to marry her. We discussed marriage, but we didn't become engaged until about a year later, and we were married a year after that, in 1980.

At the same time, Mr. Cooke sold the Lakers team—along with the Los Angeles Kings of the National Hockey League and the Forum in Inglewood, California—to Jerry

Buss, PhD. It marked a new era and a new thrust for the Lakers organization.

Dr. Buss was different—refreshingly different. A man of humble beginnings, he had earned a PhD in chemistry and amassed his fortune in real estate. In a stunning transaction, he purchased the Lakers, the Kings, The Forum, and a thirteen-thousand-acre ranch north of Los Angeles in Kern County. He preferred to wear jeans and hired basketball people to make basketball decisions. He would prove to be a *players' owner* and had some ideas that would ultimately transform the Lakers and the entire NBA. With the change in ownership came a new coach, Jack McKinney.

Coach McKinney had been with the Portland Trailblazers as an assistant to Coach Dr. Jack Ramsey (he earned a doctorate degree in education at the University of Pennsylvania) and he had been instrumental in the building and molding of their very fine team.

It was a team that the Lakers began to mirror in structure, with a strong power forward, a small forward, dual point guards, and big man in the middle.

Neither the ownership nor Coach McKinney, however, were the most important change for the Lakers' 1979–1980 campaign.

We had the number-one draft pick that year and used it to acquire a sophomore phenomenon from Michigan State University. He was a six-nine guard who was Bob Cousy, Oscar Robertson, Connie Hawkins, Elgin Baylor, and Moses Malone wrapped in one package—a nineteen-year-old kid possessing the skill set of a complete starting five of NBA Hall of Fame proportions.

He was Earvin "Magic" Johnson.

The "Showtime" Lakers

XVIII

THE SHOWTIME LAKERS

Prestidigitation /pres-te-di-je-ta-shen/: Sleight of Hand; or, Earvin "Magic" Johnson.

When Earvin entered the league, things were quite different from the Celtic dynasty era of the 1960s. More teams. More talent. More balance. There was greater difficulty in generating a dynasty. But Earvin brought the next best thing to the NBA: Showtime.

We had Kareem, the best center in basketball; Norm Nixon, a guard as good as any in the NBA; balanced scoring; and decent rebounding. But we got bounced out of the play-offs by teams that were packaged a little better.

Our fortunes shot through the moon with the 1979 NBA draft.

The debate on the best-ever player in the NBA can be an intense dialogue, but it all begins with Bill Russell, leader of the Boston Celtics who single-handedly created the concept of a sports dynasty.

By the time Earvin entered the league, things were quite different from the Celtic dynasty era of the 1960s. More teams. More talent. More balance. There was a greater difficulty to generate a dynasty. Earvin brought the next best thing to the NBA: *Showtime*.

Like Russell had done in turning a good Celtics team into a dynasty, Earvin Johnson turned a good Lakers team into an electrifying powerhouse that became an elite and entertaining NBA team. Like Russell, he brought an infectious level of intensity and intelligence. But more so than Russell or anyone else in any sport before or after, he brought a new dimension: fun.

The Showtime Lakers was a professional version of the Joe Weakley Run, Dunk, and Shoot League in Los Angeles or the Sonny Hill or Drucker Leagues on the East Coast. There were moments when it was a serious version of the Harlem Globetrotters.

Showtime showcased the talent of NBA players within the context of teamwork and team goals. Most teams had one or two stars. Other players may have had a bundle of talent but couldn't showcase it because of structured team concepts.

But with the Showtime Lakers, if you were willing to match the intensity of Earvin Johnson, if you were willing to haul ass up and down the court, and if you were willing to go hard with exuberance, you could showcase your game. In this concept, the harder the individual played, the harder the team played, and the individual leading the way was a magician, so you had to be anywhere and everywhere because you knew not from where the ball was coming—but you knew it was coming, and that was the fun part.

The Showtime Lakers was the vehicle, and Earvin Johnson was the ignition, the engine, the spark plugs, the generator, and the steering column. The vehicle had no brakes. We were the pistons providing compression that turned up pressure; we were the axles and the wheels of the vehicle. Simply put, Earvin Johnson made everybody around him a much better ball player, and we became a fine-tuned machine with high-caliber performance and passion.

He was a nineteen-year-old, six-nine point guard. In reality, he was more of a point forward. He was exciting to even the most casual basketball fan. He caught not only the attention of Los Angeles fans but also captured their imagination. He was the big box-office ticket wherever the Lakers played, and on the court, all he did was inspire the term triple-doubles, although Oscar Robertson was the undisputed master of triple-double statistics long before Earvin came on the scene. Earvin did it with passion and fun.

There was no question about who was the most exciting player in the NBA. All one had to do was look at the advanced ticket sales. Lakers games went from an occasional outing in the laid-back megalopolis that is Los Angles to must-see entertainment. And that carried over to every city in the NBA. His was the first sports jersey that became a fashion statement. Lakers games became an event that seemed to transcend basketball or sports, economic or social status, and generations and genders. A Lakers game became the place for business meetings, for aspiring actors or recording artists to make connections and, of course, dining and dating. It was a carnival of glamour, basketball, and celebrities up close. Magic was in the air.

At Everett High in Lansing, Michigan, Earvin earned the name "Magic" after a game in which he scored thirty-six points, pulled in sixteen rebounds, and had sixteen assists.

He didn't attend a perennial NCAA basketball power-house like UCLA, Louisville, Kansas, Michigan, or North Carolina. He went to Michigan State, the college closest to his home. As a freshman, he led the Spartans to a Big Ten Conference title. As a sophomore, he led the Spartans to an NCAA championship. His talent was heads and shoulders above the college level. He had to enter the draft because he simply was too good.

The Utah Jazz was supposed to pick first in the 1979 draft, but the Jazz had given up the 1979 first-round pick to the Lakers three years earlier as compensation for the free-agent signing of Gail Goodrich. The selection of Earvin "Magic" Johnson set the stage for a new benchmark season in the history of basketball.

In addition to Magic, we also added two new exceptional young players. One was Michael Cooper, who was a third-round draft choice the previous year from the University of New Mexico. He had suffered an injury during the previous year but was ready to give it a go.

The other was yet another former UCLA Bruin, Brad Holland.

There was a lot of excitement with the new ownership and coaching change. McKinney was a mellow, well-organized coach. He reminded me of the movie character Cool Hand Luke played by Paul Newman. He had a very cool and intelligent approach to the game and handling players. He brought along with him an energetic enthusiast who was also an intellectual type in Paul Westhead. Coach Westhead had been the coach at LaSalle University in Philadelphia.

But most of the excitement centered on Magic Johnson. He was coming off an NCAA championship year, having been the star in one of the most heralded NCAA buildups in college basketball history since Kareem and Elvin Hayes, when he was pitted against Larry Bird of Indiana State University in the championship game.

His personality and exuberance equaled his talent. He was an instant media star. Long before he stepped onto an NBA court, he was doing major product endorsements. He was on television across the nation and on billboards throughout Los Angeles.

Los Angeles—with its great climate, laid-back lifestyle, and movie industry—always has been able to attract high-profile players. Over the years prior to Magic, the Lakers had acquired fan favorites like Wilt Chamberlain, Kareem, Lucius Allen, Lou Hudson, and even Connie Hawkins, whose better years were a distant memory. But none had the fan or media impact of this young buck from Michigan State. Never before or since has one person entered the NBA with such a stir, including Shaquille O'Neal and LeBron James, who were unique talents with high profiles entering the NBA years later.

Before the season, Magic played with the Lakers rookie team in the summer pro league at Cal State Los Angeles. The league is designed for rookies to get a feel for the pro level and for some of the younger vets to work on some aspects of their game—or for anyone to keep in top shape during the off-season.

The capacity of the Cal State Los Angeles Field House was about 3,500. The average attendance of a summer pro-league game was about five hundred, give or take a couple or few hundred depending on who was playing. The night Magic played, making his first appearance in Los Angeles after the draft, there was sheer madness.

Not only was the Field House at capacity, but the ticket line wrapped halfway around the campus. Not just the building, but down the walkway and a campus stairway into the parking lot with cars pouring in from north, east, south, and west. It was a line that dwarfed blockbuster movie openings or rock-star concerts. Many couldn't get in.

Those who did get in were not disappointed. Magic put on a display that no one but he could have put on. His team, of course, won. It matters not the score or who else was in the show. It was all and only about Magic Johnson.

The headlines written by Ed Davis, who covered the Lakers in the *Los Angeles Sentinel* newspaper, read: "Prestidigitation: Magic Makes People Appear!" That set the tone for making people appear at NBA arenas around the country. Right off the bat, he was a bigger draw than Dr. J and Kareem. There was no way for anyone to fathom the impact he was bringing to the game. It was a miraculous blossoming of a new NBA.

Against Seattle in the play-offs, we had been beaten primarily by strong inside play but also by a big guard, six-four Dennis Johnson. And just as the Lakers had gone out to get Norm Nixon to counter the speed of Johnny Davis and Lionel Hollins of the Portland Trailblazers, there was now a need to get someone to counter the likes of DJ, as the late Dennis Johnson was known in the league. He, along with my former Warriors teammate Phil Smith and San Antonio's George Gervin, were revolutionizing the scoring-guard position, and the six-one types couldn't stop them. At six-eight (still growing to an eventual six-nine) and coming off a banner year leading Michigan State to the NCAA title against Indiana State, Magic was clearly the answer to the big-guard deficiency.

Going into the season, I had signed a new contract with the Lakers. My sister Naomi handled negotiations. By then, having served on the state attorney general's staff, she had become an established attorney in California.

In successfully negotiating my contract, she became the first female ever to negotiate a sports contract for a top-level professional athlete. Her skillful negotiating made me one of the top-paid players in the league.

We had discussed, at length, her availability and interest in representing all of my business affairs. The discussion concerned whether we wanted to jeopardize our sibling relationship with a business relationship. Throughout our lives, she had counseled me in more of a direct, you-need-to-do-this manner. Now her approach would be that of a conciliatory counselor-at-law and executive manager. I actually would have preferred her more direct approach, but the nature of the beast of being a professional athletes is that you have big-ticket business affairs in which the financial decisions rests with you. Even the smallest decisions involved five figures.

We both attended a national conference on representation of professional athletes that summer, which was sponsored by the American Law Institute. We decided to go for it, and it proved to be my best business decision during my NBA career. Going into camp that summer, everything looked good.

I had a new contract that made me very happy. I was feeling well and playing well. We had new ownership. We had a new coach. We had a sensational rookie.

Even though Magic had created a tremendous media and public stir and had a supernatural outing in his one appearance during the summer pro league, there was still the question among the team of whether this guy was for real. This was the NBA, and lying ahead of us was a grueling eighty-two game schedule. We seemingly had a solid team, with Kareem in the middle, Norm as the point guard, and Adrian and myself at the forward sports. There was a spot for him to start but not necessarily star. Obviously that's not the way Magic saw it.

There was an immense amount of pressure on him to do for the Lakers what he did at Michigan State. It seemed to me to be unfair for the public and, of course, the media to put all of that pressure on a nineteen-year-old kid.

But Magic not only could handle it, he flourished in it. He made it fun and exciting. He dealt with the challenges on the court with his multidimensional talent and with the off-court pressures with charisma and a patented smile. The guy was simply unreal. Even in the locker room, the atmosphere was upbeat.

The biggest adjustment to Magic's arrival was with Norm, who had been emerging as one of the best point guard in the league. The natural tendency and responsibility of the point guard is to *want the rock,* so Norm had no readiness to turn it over. We were headed toward a dilemma.

Norm was at his best *with the rock.* Magic was at his best *with the rock.*

But with Coach McKinney's system, the issue of one guard controlling the ball more than the other never developed. He implemented a structure that was similar to what they had at Portland, where he had been an assistant to Dr. Jack Ramsey, with two top-tier point guards—Hollins and Davis—handling the ball equally. His experience in working with two very talented point guards was fortuitous for the Lakers, as well as Norm and Magic.

That was only one element of restructuring the game plan.

Just prior to the season, Adrian was traded to Utah for Spencer Haywood. Spencer was a heralded veteran who would be counted upon to shore up our deficiency at the power-forward spot and allow me to move to small forward.

Then we acquired Jim Chones from Cleveland in exchange for Dave Robisch. Jim became our backup center to spell Kareem, and he would also spend substantial time at the big-forward position.

As we got into the season, our basic offense was the same: get the ball down low to Kareem. Basically, things hadn't changed, and again, rightly so with an NBA legend and future Hall of Famer in Kareem Abdul-Jabbar.

If Kareem was double- or tripled-teamed, as often would be the case, he could kick the ball out to me in the corner or on the wing or to Norm at the top of the key or cutting through the lane. The big forward was counted on to crash the boards, and with Magic's size, we got additional help on the boards.

In later years, Magic would become the consummate point guard, but during the 1979–1980 season, he was, perhaps, more of a surprising weapon as a banger down low that teams hadn't anticipated having to deal with. But it was as a guard sharing the ball handling with Norm that he dazzled the NBA.

Norm was quicker down the floor. Norm was a better outside shooter. Norm was quicker off the dribble to the hole. Norm played the game to textbook perfection.

Probably the biggest difference in styles of play was that Norm would out-quick defenders, and Magic would draw defenders. Magic would see over everybody while bringing the ball down court. He could handle the ball well. With his size, the defense had to respect his ability to go straight to the hoop.

Magic actually created scoring opportunities for his teammates because he forced defenders to guard him. Playing with him, you had to understand that, and you had to anticipate getting the ball. *You had to anticipate getting the ball!* The ball was coming to you if there was just a fraction for a passing lane. You may not recognize a passing opportunity, but Magic would create one without you even seeing it develop. You simply had to go to the hole and anticipate getting the ball. That's how Magic made everybody around him better. And it was fun. With Norm's speed, Magic's passing wizardry, my outside shooting, the scoring threat of Spencer, and the ultimate weapon of Kareem's finesse under the basket, we became *Showtime.*

Plus, Magic would post up opposing guards and most forwards. He could slip down as a power forward and rebound well.

Our point-guard situation was handled by emphasizing Norm for a week or two and then emphasizing Magic a week or two.

It didn't matter what part of Magic's game was emphasized. Wherever he played, he played at a superior level, night in and night out, compared to anyone else on the court. It eventually became abundantly clear that, when Magic was quarterbacking the running game, we were quite a different team. This gave Coach McKinney a heaven-sent option.

In the middle of the game, we could redefine the character of the team and the complexion of the game with just a couple of lineup changes. Out would go Kareem and Spencer, and in would come Chones and Michael Cooper.

Instantaneously, we would be transformed from a good, well-balanced team to an exciting racehorse team that was totally unparalleled in the NBA.

In any close game, the Chones-Cooper lineup insertion gave us firepower to put some quick points on the board and generate a surprising lead. Plus, Cooper was our defensive stopper who could defend either guard or forward, and sometimes center. We morphed into what seemed like an all-star team – becoming even quicker going up and down the court. Of course, Kareem was definitely *the man* for the lion's share of the game, including running at the faster tempo. It was exciting to the crowd when we morphed instantly into warp speed, and that crowd-pleasing game created what became known as the Showtime Lakers.

We knew that no matter who had the ball on the break, it was being handled proficiently. Our fast break brought about a new dimension to the NBA. And it wasn't just off missed shots or by our defense forcing a turnover; we could just as easily run a fast break when taking the ball out after the opposing team scored. That capability is what was unique and scary to other teams. It was a well-constructed team to create scoring opportunities without having to wait for the half-court opportunities to set up. Our speed and rotations would create multiple scoring opportunities before most opposing players were able to get down court. It was warp speed. It was fun. It was *Showtime*.

The system featured what we called a *turn-out rotation*.

With the turn-out rotation, if the fast break didn't materialize into an uncontested scoring opportunity, we would go into a weave-and-pick situation to get a man free under the basket. Or someone would roll off the pick for a scoring chance. Or still yet, a hesitation by the point guard during the weave and pick would sometimes lull the defender to sleep, and the point guard would simply take off down the lane for two.

If none of those plays worked, then we sometimes would just go into the half-court set. Since most of the game featured Kareem, we always had a dominant half-court set characteristic. Because we were so run-oriented, oftentimes the opposition couldn't make the complete five-man transition to defense quickly enough to stop us from a quick score as soon as we set up. We knew that was yet another possibility from the running game, and when we recognized it, we exploited it.

With the McKinney scheme, we were always in a running mode. Additionally, with a strong bench, we could run all day.

Kareem's power game was down low, but he was integral to the Showtime act. On many occasion, he would be a point center bringing the ball down the court and dishing off.

He was able to do that because he knew the system, and like Magic and Norm, he knew what everyone else was supposed to be doing. It wasn't the part of Kareem's game that sent him to the Hall of Fame but he could handle the ball well. He had great agility and no awkwardness pushing the ball down court, and once down court, the defense had to respect him as a scoring threat going to the bucket. And, as was the case in Magic's game, drawing defenders on the break created open shots for guys on the wing.

Typically, with Kareem having to battle against double- and triple-teams trying to rough him up using fifteen to twenty fouls four or five nights a week, he played the game in a very business-efficient manner. But you could see that he enjoyed Showtime as much as anyone else did, particularly when he successfully executed the break as point center. The Lakers' crowd would go crazy, and you could see that Kareem was tickled. That's a direct result of what Magic brought to the game for the fans and us as well.

The lineup with Magic, Norm, Chones, Cooper, and me became known in the locker room as the *greyhounds*. As the roster changed over the year, we became known as the original greyhounds.

Today, of course, orchestrated primary and secondary fast-break options are a part of every high school and AAU team, as well as in the pros and college. And certainly, long before Magic, teams knew how to get out on the break and fill the lanes. But in 1979, this was a whole new level to the fast-break dimension. It bears emphasis that we would fast break off a simple inbound in a matter of seconds after our opponents scored without some of the defenders being able to find the ball, until it was coming through the net at the other end of the court.

Opposing teams would score, and *before the points were registered* on the scoreboard, one of us would be scoring a bucket at the other end of the floor. This is when some of the opposing players would have their backs to the play, and often, only one or two would be back quick enough to even think about defending. What was even more amazing is that teams knew what we would do and had trouble stopping it because our personnel on the floor was uniquely gifted and well suited for this style of play.

Thus, Magic's presence on the team manifested itself in two major ways. He strengthened our inside game, and he embellished our running game. Yet another important dimension to Magic's game was that, at his size, he could box out and rebound well and, *like magic*, change from a power forward into a point guard. When Magic would get a defensive rebound, he didn't have to look for a guard to give the ball to for the start of a possible fast break. The instant he cleared the board, *it was on!*

Magic would start the break so suddenly that he would immediately eliminate two or three defenders from contesting our running game. We would already be in motion, due to our anticipation and practice, and quite frequently created a five-on-two scoring opportunity.

For our part, we would haul ass down court, knowing that a pass from Magic was apt to arrive out of nowhere. With Magic rebounding and bringing the ball down court, it put his four teammates on the run. It looked like a jailbreak. And his Hall of Fame passing was awesome. It might be a bounce pass, a lob pass, a flip over his shoulder, or a baseball strike. You had to be extremely alert for Magic's magic.

It took each of us a little while to get accustomed to Magic's magic. Fortunately, we had camp and exhibition games to find out what the deal was. There you could laugh off a bobbled pass. If you were not alert, his passes

could make you look bad. Real bad! It could make you
look like a bonehead not paying attention—like someone
who couldn't catch the ball or someone who didn't know
what to do with the ball. You didn't want to get embarrassed in front of twenty thousand people, so you learned
to become more intense.

The one guy who seemed to have more problems than
all others was Spencer Haywood.

For much of his career, Spencer had been a central
offensive-scoring figure. He was a go-to guy. Like the
Lakers and Kareem in previous years, Spencer's teams
would prefer getting into the half-court set and getting
him the rock. That was a much stronger part of his
playing than the running game.

Spencer could not make the adjustment as easily as
Kareem, for example. Kareem's overall athleticism and
ability to handle the ball made it easy for him to adapt to
the running game. But that was Kareem. Most big men
could never even think about trying to run with Magic
Johnson and could only dream of having the athleticism
to receive his passes at any split second, from any angle,
and finish the play.

Jim Chones was one of the big men who could, and
he flourished in the system. Jim, in contrast to Spencer,
found the running game just what the doctor ordered. Jim
was as proficient at handling Magic's passes as anybody.
He also did a fantastic job on defense, rebounding, and
other aspects of the game. This made Jim our fifth starter
for most of the season.

My game was immensely enhanced by our new
emphasis on running. At UCLA, the transition game

was something we worked at constantly, and it became a cornerstone of our winning. Thus, I was fundamentally well schooled on the physical and mental alertness required for challenging our opponents by transitioning rapidly from defense to offense. Our fast-break scoring opportunities were reminiscent of the Bruins' scoring opportunities created by the full-court zone press.

In a way, I was a born-again Bruin.

Game Six of 1980 NBA Finals

XIX

THROW DOWN AT THE SPECTRUM

The heck with going back to Los Angeles for game seven. We're going back to Los Angeles for a victory parade.

We opened the 1979–1980 campaign away against the San Diego Clippers in a game that set the tone for the entire season. Kareem won the game for us with a shot that just beat the final buzzer.

In a display of unbridled emotion never before seen in an opening game of a regular NBA season, Magic went berserk after Kareem's winning bucket. He seemed as excited as when he won the NCAA title at Michigan State.

He was so happy and excited that he darted straight for Kareem, leaped up, and put a headlock hug on a very surprised Kareem Abdul-Jabbar. Then he started high fiving everybody around him. It was strange. It was funny. It was exciting. We started high fiving each other.

In the NBA, there's so much of a business mentality because of all the contract issues, the competition to earn a job, trades and deals that could send you packing with little notice, and nightly competition from very large people trying to beat your brains out one elbow at a time. Playing an NBA game oftentimes is just like going to work in a coal mine. You get up, go to work, and return home. With an eighty-two-game schedule that runs six months and then an even tougher two-month play-off period, having emotions about the first game, whether you win or lose, was unheard of.

Yet there was Magic with this championship-like celebration going on. He started high fiving, and that got us all into it. We were caught off guard. We weren't so much excited about the game as much as reacting to Magic.

No one was more surprised than Kareem, who had to tell Magic to cool it because there was a long road ahead. But Magic's effervescence had already struck. Kareem and the rest of us had to subscribe to the exuberance because the alternative was to act like you didn't care about winning the game. We were happy, not quite to the level that Magic took it, but that changed instantly, and from that moment forward, we began enjoying basketball with the youthful passion of the nineteen-year-old from Lansing, Michigan. Today you see teammates congratulating each other after every victory in all sports.

The new dimension of Magic's game and the fresh air of enthusiasm and excitement brought our team close together. In contrast to guys going through an eighty-two-game grind, we became real loose.

Our pregame stretching exercises at midcourt became our *family time*. That was when we would *rag* on each other. If you were seen with a lady who didn't look or dress elegantly, the guys would get on you. If you weren't performing well or had made a dumb play recently, the guys would lay it on you heavy. This developed a sense of peer pressure that kept us on our toes while out on the court.

The greyhound squad ran right through the league and right through the preliminary rounds of the play-offs. We headed right into a showdown with the awesome record-setting Philadelphia 76ers. The Sixers matched up with us well, and were coached by Billy Cunningham. Cunningham was a former NBA all-star with the Sixers and had played alongside Chamberlain, Hal Greer, Wali Jones, Matt Goukas and Chet Walker on their 1967 championship team.

They had two great guards. There was Henry Bibby, who provided them with the same court savvy and leadership he had provided for the three UCLA Bruins NCAA championship teams as point guard. The other guard was a sensational young player in Maurice Cheeks, who could defend, score and run the show for them. Their guard play was strengthened by Eric Money and Lionel Hollins. They had a great defense-oriented center in Caldwell Jones. At one forward was a great all-around player in Bobby Jones, who played exceptional defense and was a key scoring option. Then there was The Doctor, Julius Erving. Their power on the front line came from Darryl Dawkins and Steve Mix. Rookies Jim Spanarkel,

Bernard Toone and Clint Richardson also contributed to their run to the NBA finals.

Our chameleon ability to alter our team characteristic instantaneously in the flow of the game with just a couple of player personnel changes proved too much for the Sixers. We jumped out to a three to two lead in the series.

However, tragedy struck in game five. Kareem suffered a severely sprained ankle and needed help to get off the court.

Naturally, we were worried. We were worried about the impact of the injury to Kareem's overall health. In professional sports, you are constantly aware that an injury to a key player can instantly change the fortune of any team, so you learn to live with it. When it happens, there's not a lot you can do about it. But when a major injury strikes someone you're close to, then you really do become concerned about that person's ability to spring back at some point. Never mind the game itself; you never want to see a player's career diminished for any reason, because the same could happen to you. So we were worried genuinely about Kareem's injury, because he had left the game in a bad condition.

Meanwhile, we did have a game to play and a championship series to get on with. And it appeared we'd have to do it without Kareem.

We learned that, at the minimum, he wouldn't be able to play game six in Philadelphia. It was only a remote possibility he could rejoin the team on the court for game seven in Los Angeles.

In Philadelphia, the fans were certain the momentum had shifted their way. As far as they were concerned, we could have just mailed in a loss and saved the trip across the country. Even at home, there was a big question mark about the impact of the loss of Kareem.

The greyhound group got together for a dialogue about how everybody seemingly was writing us off. We thought we might be able to sneak one past the Sixers on their home court if we *came with it*, as though we had nothing to lose.

On the plane ride to Philadelphia, Magic—along with Norm, Cooper, Chones, and myself—were fired up, and it became contagious.

At our practice preceding the game, everybody had a heightened level of intensity and sense of urgency. Even against guys who didn't get a lot of playing time were practicing just hard. We all were focused on the mission at hand. We talked it up at practice, in the locker room, at the hotel, on the bus—anywhere and to anyone who would listen, although we all were simply preaching to the choir.

It became more and more contagious.

The absence of Kareem became a rallying point. We became euphoric about the prospects of a surprise attack. We began feeling like the cat that swallowed the canary. We had something up our sleeves that not even our fans expected.

"The heck with going back to Los Angeles for game seven, we're going back to Los Angeles for a victory parade!" we said. We didn't want to just hold the fort down for Kareem; we wanted to show him how much we appreciated him by going out and going off in dedication to what he meant to our team. For all the exuberance Magic brought, Kareem was still the man!

Besides, we had to play the game without Kareem. There was no other option. So we figured we might as well go out and give them a game they would never forget.

The stage was perfectly set. Philly already was looking past game six on their home turf and ahead to game seven.

We had yet another incentive come our way.

Magic Johnson had just been insulted by the Rookie of the Year voting. The award went to Larry Bird of the Boston Celtics.

It wasn't a question of whether Larry or Magic should have won it. The issue appeared, to us, to be an incredulous discrepancy in voting. Magic lost by a wide margin!

It was a sharp slap in the face. A lesser person would have cried foul to the media or the court of public opinion. He could easily have done that because he had a case. But Magic kept that famous smile flashing and used the indignation as inspiration to show the world that he was much more deserving than the voting indicated.

With all the pregame talk among ourselves, we were *pumped*. We were sky-high for the game. We had a secret weapon: self-determination. And we had each other. We became an airtight unit.

Our only chance of winning was our greyhound game—to run like crazy. In a way, we were running scared. We knew that, without Kareem, we had to stay ahead of the posse. We had to minimize mistakes. We would run, execute, and leave the Sixers holding their jocks, trying to figure out which way we went.

We were so caught up in our enthusiasm that we actually forgot to discuss who was replacing Kareem. We just knew what we had to do in our usual roles. We never even thought about a half-court game.

What's more, we hadn't even planned on who was going to jump center. As we were concluding our pregame meeting, the issue of the tip-off came up for the first time. Coach McKinney suffered a terrible bicycle accident while out for a morning ride earlier during the season, and Coach Westhead finished up the season and took us into the play-offs. Coach Westhead asked, "Who wants to jump center?" While most of us were trying to figure out who would be most appropriate, Magic quickly volunteered.

From the tip off-to the final buzzer, it was a game fit for the Magic man. Magic scored forty-two, hitting from everywhere on the court: the pivot area, the outside, the fast break, and seemingly even from the curb out on Broad Street that runs along the side of the Spectrum in Philadelphia.

I chipped in with thirty-seven points, and we got a big game from everybody else as well. We pulled it off without the Big Fella. Playing in such a big game without Kareem is not something we would have wanted to try to do again, but we needed only this one game to win it all, and we got it. We also got strong performances from Norm Nixon, Jim Chones and Michael Cooper, while Mark Landsberger provided rebounding off the bench and little used Brad Holland chipped in with 8 points off the bench.

And we got the victory parade back in Los Angeles.

That summer, Valerie and I were married. My life was completely back on track.

XX

A FOURTH (NBA) CHAMPIONSHIP RING

Before I could really focus on the twenty-five-year, twenty-five-million-dollar Magic Johnson contract, another business matter caught my attention. It was the signing of Mitch Kupchak, who had inked a deal with the Lakers for five million dollars. Excuse me? If he is worth X amount, then I must be worth X-plus amount. My logic prevailed. I got what I wanted, and it proved to be another smart business maneuver by my sister Naomi.

Not since the great Boston Celtics teams of the sixties had an NBA team been able to repeat as champions. With our unique composition of personnel and our greyhound unit, we were the odds-on favorite to win it all again. Coach McKinney's bicycle accident kept him out for an extensive period of time the previous year, and he did not return the following year. Paul Westhead was named head coach.

We got off to a good start for the 1980–81 season. In December, however, Magic suffered torn cartilage in his knee and was out for a very long time. We played a large part of the season without him, and we were not quite the same team. Late in the season, he returned with all his youthful exuberance and looking for all of his old responsibilities.

But it was too close to the play-offs and not quite enough time for the team to make the instinctive readjustments necessary as individual players and as a basketball team to accommodate the return of the Magic man. As a result, the Houston Rockets upset us in the first round of the play-offs.

The Rockets went on to make it to the finals but were blown out by Boston, four games to two.

The following season, Magic signed a twenty-five-million-dollar contract. It was a twenty-five-year, one-million-a-year deal. It was a move that caught everyone off guard.

The loss to Houston was a shocking one, and the defeat was lingering on our minds. Then we looked up and read in the newspaper that Magic had a wonderful new contract that made him rich beyond ages.

That caused some problems.

It caused some problems with Kareem, Norm, and me. The contract gave a distinct impression that he was now part of management.

But before I could get really focused on the Magic Johnson contract, another business matter caught my attention. It was the signing of free agent Mitch Kupchak, who had just inked a deal with the Lakers for five million dollars and some change.

Naomi, in representing me, made it clear that there was no way for them to pay him all that money and expect me to be happy about the situation. She was able to successfully negotiate a contract extension that acknowledged my contributions to the team's championship level of play. Our position was sound, and our logic prevailed. At the end of the day, I got what I wanted, and it proved to be another smart business maneuver by my sister Naomi.

Magic's contract, on the other hand, ticked off a whole lot of people and caught the entire league by surprise. None of us could figure out what it all meant. Did this lengthy contract mean that he was no longer one of the boys? Given that he had a twenty-five-year deal, what was his role in the decision making? Could he decide on who was coaching? Did he have a hand in upper management? Where did all this leave Kareem, the premiere player in the league? Where did all this leave Norm, with whom he had shared point-guard responsibilities?

There were attempts to appease us when we addressed the issues head on with those involved, but a chilling effect remained in that the association between Magic and management was now stronger than the association between Magic and the team. At midseason, we found out just how powerful his contract was.

An undercurrent rift between Magic and Coach Westhead came to a head. Coach Westhead was fired.

Apparently relations between the two had been deteriorating for some time. It seemed to me to have started with the Houston play-off loss the previous year. Magic had taken the final shot of the final game. It was a potentially game-winning shot that was supposed to have been taken by Kareem as the first option or myself as the second option. Magic missed, and we were out of the play-offs.

Coaches tend to take play-off losses very badly, even worse than players, and apparently such was the case with Coach Westhead.

The tension during the season did not strike me as unusual. With a long season and so many people living and breathing so close together, things do pop up from time to time.

Usually the issue concerned our having to get the ball to Kareem. For me, that was an issue that I learned to use constructively with Adrian Dantley and, subsequently, Jim Chones by making an extra effort to get down court on the break and in position to get some points. Once we were in a half-court set, we got the ball to Kareem. That's fundamental. That's smart. Not to mention, he was the league's premier player and on his way to becoming the top scorer in the history of the game. The number-one objective was to win, and you do that by putting the ball in the basket more times than the opposition within forty-eight minutes. It didn't matter who scored; ultimately it only mattered who won.

The stuff between Magic and Coach Westhead thickened when the team became disenchanted with what we termed "over-coaching" by Coach Westhead.

He had implemented a couple of changes that negatively affected the rhythm of the running game. His intent was to enhance the running game, but in actuality, it took away from it.

Going up to Salt Lake City for a game with Utah, Magic asked me, "What do you think about what's going on, Silk?"

We exchanged some thoughts, but I was still quite unaware of the degree of Magic's disenchantment over the negative impact on our running game. Personally, I not only didn't care for the changes but also was concerned that no one liked what was going on, and I saw that as a threat to the team unity we had developed. We all enjoyed running. The team and the players were flourishing. But our concerns paled next to Magic's.

To us, running was an effective strategy. To Magic, running was his life!

The next night against Utah, it seemed that Magic played without his usual enthusiasm. Magic only played with high enthusiasm, and anything less was conspicuous and indicated that something dreadful was on his mind.

We lost the game. As we were walking off the court, Coach Westhead called Magic to the side room. That struck me as odd, because such side meetings usually took place after team meetings.

Magic emerged from the meeting wanting to be traded to a team on which he could have fun playing basketball.

Whoa! We all were surprised. The Magic man wanted out?

That, of course, was action far too drastic to an organization where Magic was not only the engine of the team on the court but also where his international public image personified the Los Angeles Lakers and *Showtime.* That meant, *see you later,* Mr. Westhead. The official statement was that the probability of a coaching change already had been contemplated.

After relieving Coach Westhead, there was an effort to get Jerry West to assume coaching duties, but he declined and recommended Pat Riley.

The issue was put to the team, and unanimously, we wanted to have Pat Riley as the interim coach. After his career with the Lakers and Phoenix Suns, Pat had been the color commentator to the play-by-play broadcasting of Chick Hearn. He was named an assistant coach to help Coach Westhead following the Jack McKinney accident.

With Patrick James Riley in, we got back on track to NBA-championship mode.

For the 1981–1982 season, the team acquired Bob McAdoo, a former NBA Rookie of the year, Most Valuable Player, and scoring champion who was en route to the Naismith Basketball Hall of Fame (2000). Bob was a prolific scorer who helped us get to four consecutive NBA finals. Bob played collegiately at the University of North Carolina and was the team's scoring leader when the Tar Heels and the UCLA Bruins team (with Henry Bibby, Larry Farmer, Bill Walton, and me) were on a collision course in the 1972 Final Four. The Florida State team we beat for the NCAA title, however, upset UNC.

We also acquired the *original* NBA "Superman," Kurt Rambis. He was drafted by the New York Knicks in 1980 out of Santa Clara University but started his pro career in Greece, leading AEK Athens to the Greek Cup Championship.

The acquisition of both McAdoo and Rambis was important because of the critical loss of Kupchak, who we unfortunately lost for the entire season

The Superman moniker came courtesy of Chick Hearn. Kurt was a mild-mannered guy off the court and actually resembled Clark Kent with his glasses on but was a tenacious bulldog when rebounding and going after loose balls. His contributions to our toughness and ability to control the inside when our defense had to make a stand were vital to our overall success.

On a personal note Valerie gave birth to our first child, a daughter named Arrianne, on September 6. Arrianne died six days later due to crib death.

With Bob McAdoo and Kurt Rambis on board, this gave us a B-12 scoring-and-energy boost, both offensively and defensively. With the dominance of Kareem, the speed of Norm, the power and passing of Magic, and the high-flying grace of Michael Cooper, *Showtime* had reloaded, and we were poised for another great run. Kareem and I averaged over twenty points a game for the season, and Magic was recording triple-doubles on almost a nightly basis. We went 50–21 under Coach Riley and 57-25 for the season. We met up with the Sixers again in the NBA Finals, winning four games to two.

The series started in Philadelphia. In game one, we fought off a twenty-seven-point effort by Julius Erving, winning 124–117, with Norm and I scoring twenty-four points each. Norm also had ten assists. In game two,

Julius wasn't being denied, leading everybody with twenty-four points and, most importantly, leading the Sixers to a 110–94 victory. Kareem had twenty-three points, and Norm again had ten assists.

Back at the Forum in Inglewood, we withstood a thirty-six-point game by Andrew Toney to win 129–108. Norm led the way with twenty-nine points. In game four, Toney came right back with twenty-eight points. Magic and I scored twenty-four points each in a 111–101 victory. Norm had fourteen assists as we went up three games to one.

We returned to the Spectrum in Philly and had no better luck with Toney. He had thirty-one points as the Sixers won big, 135–102. Bob McAdoo had a nice game for us, with twenty-three points. Norm had thirteen assists. The Sixers' center, Darryl Dawkins, with his "Chocolate Thunder" helped his team with twenty points and muscled Kareem pretty good on the defensive end. Kareem came back strong with an all-around active game leading us to a championship victory. Bob had a tremendous game with sixteen points, nine rebounds, and three spirited blocked shots. Magic had a triple-double in points (thirteen), assists (thirteen), and rebounds (thirteen) and was named MVP. I led the team with twenty-seven points in the championship victory. Julius got thirty for the Sixers. For the series, I led the team in scoring, averaging 19.7, with five others also averaging double figures: Kareem with 18, Norm with 17.7, Bob with 16.3, Magic with 16.2, and Michael Cooper with 13.3. Norm and Magic had double-double averages, with Magic also averaging 10.8 rebounds a game, and Norm averaging ten assists a game.

XXI

CHANGING OF THE GUARD

Frankly, as I sat on the bench sidelined during much of the 1985 championship series against Boston and watched James Worthy emerge as a brilliant NBA performer, I saw the writing on the wall. I thought that if my knee could come back strong, I could contribute to the rotation. But I wasn't even close.

It is said that the only thing that's certain in life is change. The following year, Pat Riley was named head coach. This would be the fourth Lakers coach in five years.

Coach Riley was great. With Riley in, we got back to our winning ways, and that refueled Showtime. We had a great year. And we had a great young talent selected as the number-one pick in the draft: James Worthy from North Carolina. In the sports vernacular, he was a horse. He was big, fast, quick, intelligent, and athletically domineering; he was a scorer, a defender, a team player, and a quality fit for a Lakers team that could morph into a higher gear in a nanosecond or generate a powerful low-post half-court game. James was a man for all seasons.

We made it to the NBA finals again, and again it was against the Philadelphia 76ers. But this was a much-improved version of the Sixers. They had added Moses Malone. And they needed no incentive to throw everything they had at us. They knew what we had done to them before—twice.

They finally rose to the occasion and got their revenge. They swept us in four straight. The sweep was tough and left us with an empty feeling, but the silver lining in this dark cloud was that that Julius Erving – the Doctor – won his first NBA championship and that was something to which we could tip our hat.

Since we were blown out with a sweep, the loss was not as bad as it might have been in a close series where it's nip-and-tuck and you're beating up on each other for a week and a half, riding an emotional roller-coaster on rails of anxiety.

At the outset of the following season, 1983–1984, Norm Nixon was traded to the Los Angeles Clippers in exchange for my former UCLA teammate Swen Nater and the rights to Byron Scott.

Byron was the Clippers' first-round draft choice and the first guard chosen. He had attended Arizona State University. He was a local kid out of Inglewood,

California, growing up in the shadows of the Forum. He modeled his game after Jerry West.

The Norm Nixon trade was a difficult one for me to swallow. It's one thing if a guy leaves as a free agent—you're happy for him, thinking he's better off or at least got a better deal—but another if he is traded away. Norm was an exceptional teammate. We not only were compatible running mates on the court, but he helped elevate the speed of my game. For the previous five years, it was Kareem, Norm, and me. Magic and Cooper came along and made it a quintet for four of those years, as we emerged as the Showtime Lakers and made it synonymous with exciting, fast-pace basketball. No matter who won the championship in those years, we were the most exciting team in basketball.

Norm was a leader, and all of us were good friends with him, including Magic. The fans loved Norm. At his first game back at the Forum, fans gave him a tremendous, thunderous, heartfelt standing ovation that lasted a full five minutes. The magnificence of the moment was the love of the Lakers fans for Norm amidst their understanding the trade was just a part of the world of professional sports.

That year, toward the end of the season, I became violently ill with what was described as a parasitic infection. I tried to get back into the flow of things for the play-offs, but as was the case with Magic two years prior, there was too little time for me to get back to my usual game. We lost to Boston in the finals at the fabulous Forum.

The following year turned out to be even worse. I suffered an awful knee injury in a midseason collision with Ernie Grunfeld of the New York Knicks. I was again sidelined for a substantial portion of the season.

Both of my extended periods of absence gave James Worthy a golden chance to show what he could do at small forward. With his strong inside game, he had been drafted principally as a power forward. But my absence created an opening in the Lakers' lineup, and James did more than fill it, he strengthened it. He established himself as an up-and-comer in the NBA and was a catalyst in the team's championship campaign that year.

Once again, I struggled to come back near the end of the season, but I could only get to about 60 percent of my true playing form. But with James performing well in a starting role, there was no big concern for pushing me into the rotation. As a result, I sat out mostly and watched while we went on to win the championship.

At the outset of the 1985–1986 basketball season, with James firmly established and my injured knee still in question, there was an opportunity for the Lakers to create some salary-cap room to sign AC Green, who was the new number-one pick, and I was placed on waivers. I was now an eleven-year veteran trying to bounce back from what is usually a career-ending injury.

Frankly, as I sat on the bench sidelined during much of the 1985 championship series against Boston and watched James Worthy emerge as a brilliant NBA performer, I saw the writing on the wall. I thought that if my knee could come back strong, I could contribute to the rotation. The bad news was that I wasn't even close to contributing, but good news was that the Lakers finally beat the Celtics in the NBA finals, winning it on their home floor, four games to two.. At the end of the day, all that mattered was that it felt great to beat the Celtics, even if playing a lesser role than in my previous years with the Lakers. As an organization, we got the monkey off our back.

I got the call from Jerry West, who informed me of the planned move. Because of my popularity in the Los Angeles area, they wanted to handle things very carefully. We had a big emotional press conference that marked the end of my tenure as a Laker and signaled the end of my NBA career.

Jerry had informed that there were a few teams interested in me. There was some interest expressed by the New York Knicks and Chicago Bulls. And then, of course, there was the Los Angeles Clippers.

Although I could see the waiver situation approaching, I was not really prepared to deal with opportunities to play elsewhere. Retiring was really the main consideration. I had been well advised by my managing group, so I was prepared to make the transition to private life.

On the other hand, even with a debilitating knee problem, I wasn't ready to hang it up. If I could get the knee straightened out and get in some good workouts, I'd be good to go. All I had to do was figure out which situation could work best for me.

Former Lakers' assistant coach Stan Albeck was the head coach at Chicago. I really thought about going there. But with my family just starting, the prudent thing for me to do was stay in Los Angeles.

The Clippers had acquired Cedric Maxwell, one of the elite NBA players who played at full tilt at all times and led Boston to a couple of championships. They had also drafted a seven-footer, Benoit Benjamin, from Creighton University. Then there were Norm Nixon and Marques Johnson, two premier NBA players and two of my personal friends.

Although there were some age and ailment issues with Norm, Marques, Cedric, and myself, there were signs that this team had the potential of making the play-offs if we didn't break down all at once or at too many inconvenient times of the season. Every team I had played on since high school made the play-offs, which minimally said your team was one of the best. Postseason play was the barometer by which I gauged my decision of whether to continue playing.

The Clippers also had a good young coach in Don Chaney. I thought certainly the ingredients were there and that my presence might be a key factor to help them get to the promised land of postseason action.

But Murphy's Law had the upper hand on the *ifs* concerning the age and ailments: *if* my knee comes around, I could give some quality time; *if* Marques could have another one of his stellar seasons; *if* Cedric could overcome his late-career injuries and stay healthy; *if* Norm could stay healthy, he had all the tools to lead the Clippers to a play-off spot in the Western Conference. It would have taken a miracle for all of those *ifs* to fall into place, and as it turned out, it was too much of a long shot.

We got off to a good start, and then the wheels started falling off the wagon. My knee wasn't worth a plum nickel. Actually, the knee felt fine, but I did not have the same explosion, and ability to explode in any professional sport determines success. If your explosiveness is limited, your success will be limited. Added to the knee problem, I severely sprained an ankle. It was an injury in which I would never fully recover. When you are younger, you can try to make it to another season. But when you are in what very well may be your last season, it is a career-threatening injury.

Cedric was at the end of the line. Marques and Norm started ailing, and we didn't have enough reserve power to allow them the rest they needed. We spiraled downward into the cellar. The only bright spot was the late Derek Smith, a third-year player out of the University of Louisville, who was a member of Coach Denny Crum's 1980 NCAA championship team.

With the inability to perform at the level to which I was accustomed, I made the decision to move on and make the adjustment to private life. We were not a championship-caliber team, but we had a nice enough nucleus to try and make some noise if this, that, or the other could happen—or, as the colloquial saying goes, if the creek doesn't rise. But there was no good fortune to come about for us.

On December 25, 1985, I publicly announced my retirement from the National Basketball Association.

PASTOR AND FIRST LADY - Second Baptist Church of Santa Monica, California, pastor and first lady Rev. Leo Leander Wilkes and Thelma Naomi (Benson) Wilkes. Rev. Wilkes retired in 2004 from the ministry, as Pastor Emeritus and his legacy was read into the United States Congressional Record.

EPILOGUE

Toward the end of my basketball years, I was blessed with the birth of two wonderful children, a daughter, Sabreen, and a son, Omar. Valerie and I were blessed again with a third child after my career, a son, Jordan Keith, in the summer of 1987.

The blessing of children has a way of making one reflect on life...where you've been and where you're going.

For me, it's taken me back to my family origins and upbringing, and as I reflect through the years—my successes and shortcomings—the one thing that's been with me through it all has been my spiritual outlook.

Through my years of questioning, failures, challenges, introspection, and subsequent adoption of the Islamic faith, I still held on to Jesus Christ. Even though I felt warm with Islam, and I feel an affinity to all religions today, my belief in the almighty and in the finer qualities of humankind are bolstered by a practical awareness of

Christ consciousness. Perhaps his holiness, the Dalai
Lama, a Buddhist monk, said it best when asked about
his religion: "My religion is very simple. My religion is
kindness."

For that strength, which may not have always been
obvious, I have my family, teachers, coaches, mentors,
and others to thank. My father and mother provided the
physical and mental nurturing, combined with many
lessons learned along the way that helped me to make
the tough choices, deal with adversities, and manage
success.

In the mid-1980s, I first learned that Naomi had been
diagnosed with a terminal illness in 1978 and had been
given five years to live. In subsequent years following
her transition, in 1993, I talked about many things with
my family and returned to using Keith, my birth middle
name, and retained Jamaal as my first name.

I like to think that the many accolades I have received
for having an even-tempered, team-oriented demeanor
simply reflects my father's influence, and, of course, was
later augmented by the wisdom of Coach John Wooden.
I also like to think that my selection into the Naismith
Basketball Hall of Fame gave our family two Hall of
Famers, my father, whose forty-five years in the sacred
art earned him a place in the Congressional Record, and
my fifteen years in college and professional basketball
that earned me enshrinement in 2012.

If I were honored with an opportunity to pass along a thought or two that young people may care to subscribe to, it would be to understand the role that family plays in our lives. Though it may sometimes, in some of our lives, not seem positive, we must keep in mind that our family members are motivated by love and concern for our well-being.

Secondly, I encourage education. Education is the key to unlocking many doors. Without this key, you may find yourself locked out. A commitment to education is a commitment to yourself...to make your dreams a reality and become the best possible person you can become. Expand your concept of education to be open to all types of learning—learn from others, learn from situations you encounter, and learn from your own mistakes and failures.

And finally, if I may repeat an age-old saying, "Do unto others as you would have others do unto you." Life is too short, and oftentimes too complicated, for unwise decisions. There is a good life ahead when we are willing to invest our beliefs in good principles and invest our actions in activities that demonstrate good character.

Hall of Famer Jamaal Keith Wilkes

SPECIAL ACKNOWLEDGEMENTS AND THANKS

G rowing up in a home of faith, I've always been humbled by God's grace and movements in my life and the people who have meant so much in so many ways.

I've already spoken in these memoirs of my immediate family. There are also Valerie's parents, Mr. and Mrs. Vernon Topping (deceased), and a host of extended family members. There have been many others—family and friends—far too many to mention here. I would be remiss if I did not include Mr. and Mrs. Bob Swanson and their son John and daughters Terri, Wendy, and Barbara; Mr. and Mrs. Jack Trigueiro; and the late coach and Mrs. John Wooden among my extended family.

I also wish to publicly thank my church families at Olivet Baptist Church in Ventura, California, and Second Baptist Church in Santa Barbara, California, whose guidance was important to me at pivotal points in my youth and young-adult years. Of course, my collegiate and NBA basketball careers have been awesome blessings for my family and me.

I have written and spoken much of Bill Walton, one of my closest and dearest friends for over forty years. Bill along with Kareem Abdul-Jabbar, Earvin Johnson, Rick Barry, Pat Riley, and the late John Wooden were instrumental in having me immortalized in the Naismith Basketball Hall of Fame. UCLA athletic director Dan Guerero and Bill Bennett presented my official nomination, and Los Angeles Times sportswriter Jerry Crowe and Los Angeles Laker communications executive John Black also played pivotal roles.

Basketball is a team sport, and my teammates from the Ventura Youth League through high school, college, and the NBA are far too many to mention. Every season, every practice, and every game plan involved many athletes and coaches—beginners, amateur legends, and superstars. To each person, I am thankful.

In my post-career business endeavors, I have been blessed with the friendship and support of Liza Wayne for more than a decade.

Finally, and not least, there's my friend, coauthor, and editor, the affable Edward Davis. Ed has been a longtime personal friend and business representative. Many thanks.

ABOUT THE COAUTHOR...

Edward Reynolds Davis, Jr. is a five-time National Newspaper Publishers Association award-winning writer. His journalism career spans forty-plus years in news reporting and public affairs in private and public sectors. He is a double major graduate of California State University, Northridge, and seminary alumnus of the Interdenominational Theological Center - Morehouse School of Religion. He is a native of Pittsburgh, Pennsylvania, and now resides in Marietta, Georgia.

Made in the USA
Coppell, TX
15 March 2024

30102990R10184